North Country
CABIN
COOKING

More than 300 quick 'n' easy, sure-to-please
recipes for your cabin kitchen

by **Margie Knoblauch**
and **Mary Brubacher**

Adventure Publications, Inc.
Cambridge, MN

Dedication

We dedicate this book, with love and gratitude, to those who have generously shared their recipes with us . . . and to our families, the ultimate taste-testers.

10 9 8 7 6 5 4 3 2

Published by Adventure Publications, Inc. (formerly published by Garlic Press)
820 Cleveland Street South
Cambridge, MN 55008
800-678-7006
www.adventurepublications.net
All rights reserved
Printed in U.S.A.

ISBN: 978-1-59193-283-3

Table of Contents

Introduction

"Going to the cabin" is a common phrase in the Upper Mid-west. On weekends and holidays, we "cabin people," looking for a change of pace, flock to the North Country's lakes and forests. Too often, however, we work just as hard cooking at the cabin as we do at home.

We want to be proud of the food we serve, but we want to be "on vacation," too. The recipes we present here are intended to make time spent at the cabin enjoyable for everyone—including the cook. Many of these recipes can be made at home and taken to the cabin. Others are one-dish meals that can be prepared easily in the cabin kitchen. All are geared for the vacationer or weekend "cabin person."

We requested recipes from friends and relatives who have cabins, and from others who understand the need for more casual cook-ing while vacationing. We asked for recipes that are tasty and popular, can be made in advance and conveniently transported, are easy to prepare, and use ingredients that are readily available—even in small, out-of-the-way grocery stores and markets.

In gathering these recipes, we learned that most of us, when going to the cabin for a short time, prepare food at home and take it with us. By doing so, we can enjoy our leisure time and still have delicious "home-cooked" meals.

Organization is the key to having that leisure time. Plan menus and prepare food in advance, whenever possible. Measure and mix dry ingredients for a recipe at home, especially if that recipe requires spices or seasonings not stocked at the cabin. Put the mixture into a plastic bag or other container, and label it accordingly.

Sharing cooking responsibilities also helps ensure leisure time for everyone. When a cabin is being shared by two or more families, each family can be responsible for a meal. Have a group of young people? Use a "kaper chart," as the Scouts do, to assign meal-time tasks.

Planning ahead, sharing kitchen duties, and using the recipes presented here should greatly reduce the amount of time spent is cabin kitchens preparing meals.

To those who contributed these recipes, we extend a heartfelt "thank you." To the reader, we express our hopes that this cookbook helps "cabin cooks" everywhere have more time to relax and enjoy those golden days in the North Country.

Appetizers & Snacks

Curry Dip

Great for a party or when just relaxing at home.

1⅓ cups Hellmann's
mayonnaise

2 tablespoons honey

2 tablespoons ketchup

2 tablespoons grated onion

Dash of salt

1 tablespoon lemon juice

7 drops Tabasco sauce

1 teaspoon curry powder

Combine all of the ingredients. Serve with fresh vegetables. You can use cauliflower, green pepper, celery, carrots, tomatoes, mushrooms, etc.

Nacho Dip

An easy snack, or appetizer, for a group.

2 1-pound cans refried beans

1 large onion, chopped
and sautéed

1 4-ounce can chopped
green chilies, drained

1 11-ounce bottle mild
taco sauce

1 pound shredded
cheddar cheese

1 pound shredded
Monterey Jack cheese

Layer ingredients in order listed in a 9-by-13-inch pan.

Bake at 325° for 25 minutes. Dip into it with nachos, crackers, etc.

Baked Cheese Dip

So simple to make, and so good.

1 cup mayonnaise
(not low-calorie)

1 cup sharp cheddar
cheese, grated

1 medium onion, cut
very fine, or grated

Mix all ingredients. Put in a shallow oven dish or 9-inch pie plate. For color, you may sprinkle with paprika or parsley.

Bake at 400° until brown, 15 to 20 minutes. Do not over-bake. Serve with crackers or fresh vegetables. Recipe may be doubled for a large group.

Rye and Dip

Make dip at home and take it with you. Prepare bread at last minute.

1-pound loaf unsliced
rye bread

⅔ cup sour cream

⅔ cup mayonnaise
(not salad dressing)

1 teaspoon dill weed or
dill seed

1 teaspoon Beau Monde
seasoning

1 tablespoon onion flakes

1 tablespoon parsley

Cut oval or rectangular hole in top of bread. Remove this bread, and break into bite-sized chunks. Make dip out of remaining ingredients. Refrigerate overnight.

Fill loaf with dip and surround with bread chunks for dipping. (You may want to double the dip recipe.)

Dip for Raw Vegetables

2 cups sour cream (or 1 cup sour cream and 1 cup mayonnaise)

1 package Knorr's vegetable soup mix

¼ teaspoon curry, optional

Combine ingredients.

Refrigerate for at least 1 hour before serving with chips or fresh vegetables.

Chopped Vegetable Spread

Great with Wheat Thins. If you have a food processor, the chopping will be a snap!

1 cup chopped celery

1 green pepper, chopped

1 small onion, chopped

1 large cucumber, chopped

1 package unflavored gelatin

2 cups mayonnaise

1 teaspoon salt

Drain juice from vegetables. Mix gelatin with ¼ cup cold water. Add ¼ cup boiling water. Mix with mayonnaise and salt. Mix into vegetables. Chill.

Salmon Spread

Men really like this one.

8 ounces cream cheese, softened

1 16-ounce can salmon (pink or red), drained, flaked and deboned

1 tablespoon lemon juice

tablespoon grated onion

¼ teaspoon liquid smoke

¼ teaspoon salt

Snipped parsley

Combine all ingredients, except parsley. Refrigerate for 8 hours.

Serve in small glass bowl or make a "mound" on a plate. Sprinkle with snipped parsley. Serve with Kavli (Norwegian flat bread) or plain crackers.

Zucchini-Cheese Spread

4 small or 2 medium
zucchini, peeled and
shredded

1 tablespoon diced onion

3 cups grated cheese
(cheddar, Colby, etc.)

Salt and pepper to taste

In ovenproof dish (approxi-
mately 8-inches-by-5-inches)
layer half of the zucchini, half
of the onion, salt and
pepper and half of the cheese.
Repeat layering.

Bake, at 350°, only until
cheese melts, about 8 minutes.
Serve with crackers.

Quick Shrimp Spread

8 ounces cream cheese,
softened

1 bottle chili sauce

1 6½-ounce can of tiny
shrimp, drained

On a shallow dish, like a small
platter, spread cream cheese.
Cover with chili sauce—you
may not need an entire bottle.
Put shrimp on top of this.
Serve with crackers.

Two Easy Cream Cheese Appetizers

1 package cream cheese,
rolled in lemon pepper

1 package cream cheese,
topped with peach chutney

Serve with crackers.

Cheese Balls

Great for camping. Do ahead and freeze.

1 8-ounce package cream cheese, softened

1 small jar pimento, cut up

1 4-ounce package smoky flavored cheddar cheese, shredded

½ cup butter or margarine, softened

½ teaspoon salt

Garlic salt

2 tablespoons minced onion

Worcestershire sauce

Chopped nuts or parsley

Mix all ingredients in an electric mixer. Form into 3 balls. Roll in chopped nuts or parsley. Place in refrigerator until firm. Wrap and freeze.

Serve with crackers.

Hot Triscuit Hors D'oeuvres

Good and easy.

4 ounces shredded mozzarella cheese

4 ounces cheddar cheese, shredded

half of a 6-ounce can black olives, chopped

6 green onions (with tops), finely chopped

½ cup Hellmann's mayonnaise

Combine and mix all ingredients. Spread on Triscuits.

Bake at 375° for 7 minutes.

Hot Dried Beef Appetizer

1 8-ounce package
   cream cheese
½ cup sour cream
3 tablespoons milk
1 2½-ounce jar
   chipped beef
¼ cup minced green pepper
½ teaspoon garlic salt
2 tablespoons horseradish
½ cup chopped nuts

Beat cheese, sour cream and milk with mixer until well blended. Add remaining ingredients, except nuts. Pat into a buttered, 8-by-8-inch baking dish. Top with nuts.

Bake at 350° for 20 minutes. Serve with crackers. May be prepared ahead of time and baked later.

Howie's Dill Pickle Special

1 medium jar dill pickles
1 2½-ounce jar dried beef
1 package cream cheese,
   either size, depending
   on how many servings
   you desire

Soften cream cheese. Dry pickles with paper towels. Spread slice of dried beef with cream cheese to the edge.

Roll dried beef around pickle, with cream cheese next to the pickle. Insert toothpicks through each pickle at ½-inch intervals. Slice the wrapped pickles into ½-inch pieces. Cover.

Refrigerate until serving time.

Taco Dip Hors D'oeuvres

It's a winner! Even those who are not Mexican food fans love it.

1 8-ounce package cream cheese, softened

1 8-ounce carton sour cream

⅛ teaspoon garlic salt

½ head lettuce, shredded

⅔ cup chopped onion

¼ cup chopped green pepper

2 tomatoes, chopped

1 cup cheddar cheese

2 teaspoons pitted black olives

Taco sauce

Combine cream cheese, sour cream and garlic salt. Mix well. Spread on shallow plate. Place in refrigerator for 15 minutes.

Sprinkle lettuce, onion, green pepper and tomatoes over the cheese mixture. Sprinkle cheese and olives over entire mixture. Dot with taco sauce, just before serving. Serve with taco chips for dipping. Can be prepared early in the day.

Mini-Pizza

A snack or appetizer.

Ritz or Triscuit crackers

Slices of cheese singles, cut into quarters

Tomato sauce

Pepperoni slices

Layer in order listed.

Bake at 350° for 3 to 5 minutes.

Dill Squares

Combine the butter mixture with cheese at home,
and refrigerate until needed at your destination.

¼ pound (½ cup) butter, softened

¼ teaspoon Tabasco sauce

¼ teaspoon Worcestershire sauce

¼ teaspoon onion powder

2 teaspoons dill weed

Dash of cayenne

1 5-ounce jar Old English cheese

1 loaf Pepperidge Farm very thin, white bread

Blend first 6 ingredients Add cheese. Mix well. Spread slice of bread with the butter-cheese mixture. Put second slice of bread on top. Spread cheese mixture on top of this slice, also. Trim crusts from "sandwich," and cut each into 6 squares. *This must be cut before baking.* Place on cookie sheet.

Bake at 350° for 15 minutes, or until brown.

North Country Seafood Cocktail

This one will fool your relatives from the sea coast.
It's a great way to use leftover cooked fish—sunnies, crappies,
bluegills, northerns or walleyes.

Pre-cooked fish

Seafood cocktail sauce

Shredded lettuce (optional)

Lemon slices (optional)

Break fish into bite-sized pieces, removing skin and bones. Mix with cocktail sauce. Serve individually in a cup or small glass as an appetizer, or on shredded lettuce with lemon as a garnish.

Bite-Sized Stuffies

You will love this one.

1 loaf frozen bread dough, thawed

36 stuffed green olives, cubes of ham, cheese or shrimp

Butter

Thaw dough overnight in refrigerator. Cut thawed dough into 36 pieces with scissors. Shape each piece around meat, olive, cheese or shrimp. Seal well. Place on greased cookie sheet. Cover and let rise until puffy.

Bake at 400° for 10 to 12 minutes. Brush with plain or garlic butter.

May be prepared in the morning to be baked later in the day. Place on greased cookie sheet in refrigerator. Let rise at room temperature at least ½ hour before baking.

Gorp

A nutritious snack, easy to make.
Packable and portable for the outdoor enthusiast.

Raisins
Dry roasted peanuts
Sunflower seeds, shelled
Slivered almonds

Choose one of the following:
M&M's candies
Reese's peanut butter pieces
Carob chips
Chocolate chips

Mix equal parts of all ingredients. Store in covered container or plastic bag.

Caramel Corn

2 bags Old Dutch Puffcorn
2 cups brown sugar
1 cup margarine
½ cup light corn syrup
1 teaspoon vanilla
Pinch of salt
½ teaspoon baking soda

Combine brown sugar, mar-garine, corn syrup, vanilla and salt in saucepan. Boil for 5 minutes, stirring often. Remove from heat and stir in baking soda. Pour over Puffcorn in a large roaster, and stir well.

Bake at 250° for 1 hour, stirring every 15 minutes. Cool on a cookie sheet or tin foil.

Breads & Breakfasts

Susie's Simple Beer Bread

3 cups self-rising flour

1 can of beer, at room temperature

4 tablespoons sugar

Combine ingredients. Mix well. Pour into well-greased bread pan.

Bake at 350° for 45 minutes. Makes great toast, too!

Prairie Brown Bread

A wonderful, hearty quick bread that freezes well.

4 cups whole wheat flour

1⅓ cups all-purpose flour

1 quart buttermilk

2 cups brown sugar

4 teaspoons baking soda

1 teaspoon salt

Thoroughly mix all ingredients. Pour batter into greased bread pans. This will make 2 large, or 4 small, loaves.

Bake large loaves at 350° for 1 hour. Check small loaves after 40 minutes. Remove from pans to cool on rack.

Strawberry Bread

Freezes well.

3 cups flour

2 cups sugar

1 teaspoon baking soda

1½ teaspoons cinnamon

1 teaspoon salt

1 3-ounce package strawberry JELL-O

4 eggs, beaten

1 16-ounce package frozen strawberries, thawed

1¼ cups butter or margarine, softened

1¼ cups chopped walnuts

Sift dry ingredients, including JELL-O, into a large bowl. Make a "well" in this mixture. Mix other ingredients in a small bowl, then pour into "well" and stir by hand. Pour into greased and floured loaf pans.

Bake at 350° for about 1 hour, until inserted toothpick comes out clean. Makes 5 very small loaves (3-by-5-inch size). Can use larger pans, and bake accordingly.

Banana Blueberry Bread

Keeps in the refrigerator for weeks.

3 cups unsifted flour

1½ cups sugar

4 teaspoons baking powder

1 teaspoon salt

1½ cups quick-cooking oats

⅔ cup vegetable oil

4 eggs, slightly beaten

2 cups mashed bananas

2 cups fresh or frozen blueberries

Mix flour, sugar, baking powder and salt. Stir in oats. Add oil, eggs, bananas and blueberries, stirring just until mixed. Pour batter into 2 greased 8½-by-4½-inch loaf pans.

Bake at 350° for about 60 minutes. Let cool in pan for 10 minutes, then remove from pan to a wire rack. When cool, wrap and refrigerate for several hours before slicing.

Monkey Bread

The aroma of this bread will act as a magnet for anyone in your cabin, including the cook.

4 7½-ounce tubes refrigerated buttermilk biscuits

1 cup sugar

1 teaspoon cinnamon

1 cup brown sugar

¾ cup margarine

Cut each biscuit into quarters. Mix sugar and cinnamon. Dip biscuit pieces into sugar mixture or shake in a plastic bag. Put pieces in a well-greased angel food pan or Bundt pan.

Melt brown sugar and margarine. Do not boil. Pour over pieces in cake pan.

Bake at 350° for about 30 minutes. Let cool for 10 minutes, then turn upside down on a plate. Tear off pieces, or cut into slices.

Very Lemon Bread

Freezes well.

½ cup shortening

1 cup sugar

Grated rind of a lemon

2 eggs

½ cup milk

1½ cups flour

1 teaspoon baking powder

¾ teaspoon salt

¼ cup sugar

Juice of 1 lemon

Cream shortening and sugar. Add lemon rind. Beat in eggs. Sift dry ingredients. Add alternately with milk to first mixture.

Bake in 9-by-5-inch loaf pan at 350° for 50 to 60 minutes. Remove from pan while warm.

Mix sugar and lemon juice. Spoon over the bread. Prick the top with a fork, so bread will absorb the juice.

Blue Cheese Bread

1 loaf French bread, sliced about 1-inch thick

½ cup butter

¼ cup blue cheese, crumbled

¼ teaspoon salt

⅛ teaspoon pepper

Combine butter, cheese, salt and pepper. Spread on each slice of French bread. Wrap bread in foil.

Bake at 400° for 20 minutes. Serve hot.

Swedish Hard Tack

Similar to flat bread, but tastier, we believe.
Serve it "for coffee," with salads, or just to eat anytime.

¾ cup butter

½ cup sugar

2 cups cracked wheat
(quick-cooking oatmeal
may be substituted)

3 cups white flour

1 teaspoon salt

1 teaspoon baking, soda

1½ cups buttermilk

Cream butter and sugar. Mix dry ingredients. Add to creamed mixture, alternating with buttermilk. Form into balls the size of small baseballs Cover and let "rest" for about 1 hour. Roll thin as for pie crust.

Bake on cookie sheets for 15 minutes at 375°. Watch closely near end of baking time—when it starts to brown, remove from oven. When cool, break into pieces and store in airtight container.

Whipped Cream Biscuits

Only two ingredients in these quick, light biscuits!

½ pint whipping cream

1¼ cups self-rising flour

Whip cream until it forms soft peaks. Add self-rising flour. Mix. Drop by tablespoonful onto ungreased cookie sheet.

Bake at 375° for about 10 minutes, or until light brown.

Makes 12 biscuits.

Celery Loaf
A unique way to fix bread.

1-pound loaf unsliced
   white bread
½ cup butter or margarine,
   softened
1 teaspoon celery seed
¼ teaspoon salt
¼ teaspoon paprika
Dash of cayenne pepper

Trim crusts from top, sides and ends of loaf. Mix remaining ingredients. Spread over top of loaf. Cut loaf at 1-inch intervals from the top almost to the bottom crust. Spread mixture sparingly over both sides of slits. Place on cookie sheet.

Bake at 400° for 15 to 18 minutes, or until golden brown. Before serving, cut l oaf through to the bottom.

If you wish to make ahead of time, cover with wax paper and refrigerate until time to bake.

Beer Muffins
These muffins are quick and easy and have a certain pizzazz!

2 cups Bisquick
2 tablespoons sugar
1 cup beer
4 ounces (about 1 cup)
   shredded cheddar cheese
   (optional)

Mix all ingredients. Fill greased muffin cups ⅔ full of batter. Let stand at least 10 minutes.

Bake at 375° for 15 minutes.

Makes 12 muffins.

Parmesan Toast

This is especially good as an appetizer or served with salads.
Watch out . . . it's addictive.

1 loaf baguette French bread
(smaller in diameter than
regular French bread)
1 pound butter, melted
8-ounce can Parmesan cheese

Slice baguette French bread into ¼-inch slices. Quickly dip each side in melted butter, then in Parmesan cheese. Place in jelly roll pan.

Bake at 325°. After about 8 minutes, drain any unmelted butter from pan, and turn each slice over. Continue baking for another 8 minutes. Remove from pan and put on paper towels to absorb any excess butter.

You may need slightly more than 1 pound butter or 8 ounces of Parmesan, depending on the size of the bread loaf. Store in airtight container. It freezes beautifully.

Scandia Valley Skillet Biscuits

2 tablespoons butter
1 cup buttermilk
¼ teaspoon baking soda
½ teaspoon salt
1¾ cups flour
1 tablespoon baking powder

Melt butter in 8-inch iron skillet. Remove excess butter, and set aside for later use. In a small bowl, stir soda into buttermilk. Combine dry ingredients in another bowl. Mix well. Add this to the buttermilk; stir only until moistened and mixed well.

Knead on floured board about 15 times. Press dough to 1-inch thickness. Cut with floured cutter. Place biscuits in skillet, and spoon remaining butter over top of biscuits.

Bake at 450° for 12 to 15 minutes, or until biscuits are medium brown. Serve hot.

Makes about 8 biscuits.

Thumbprint Pastries

1 10-ounce can refrigerated big flaky biscuits

½ cup sugar

1 teaspoon cinnamon

¼ cup butter or margarine, melted

Jam or preserves (jelly is too thin)

Combine sugar and cinnamon. Dip both sides of each biscuit into melted butter, then in sugar-cinnamon mixture. Make deep thumbprint in center of each roll. Fill with 1 teaspoon jam.

Bake in ungreased 9-by-13-inch pan, or jelly roll pan, at 375° for 15 to 20 minutes, or until golden brown.

Makes 10 pastries.

Sour Cream Coffee Ring
Freezes well.

½ cup margarine or butter

1 cup sugar

2 eggs

1 cup sour cream

1 teaspoon vanilla

2 cups flour

1 teaspoon baking soda

1 teaspoon baking powder

1 teaspoon salt

¼ cup brown sugar

Topping

½ cup chopped nuts

½ cup brown sugar

2 teaspoons cinnamon

Cream margarine and sugar. Add eggs. Mix. Add remaining ingredients. Put half the batter into a greased 10-inch tube pan. Sprinkle with half the topping. Repeat.

Bake at 350° for 45 to 50 minutes.

Swedish Kringler Coffee Cake

Delicious.

1 cup flour
½ cup butter
1–2 tablespoons water

Mix flour, butter and water, as for pie crust. Press into a jelly roll pan (11-by-16-inch), or press into two 4-inch-wide strips the length of a cookie sheet (this choice would be baked on a cookie sheet).

1 cup water
½ cup butter
1 cup flour
3 eggs
1 teaspoon almond extract

Heat the water and butter to boiling. Remove from heat. Stir in flour, beating until smooth. Add the 3 eggs, 1 at a time, and beat until smooth after each one. Add almond extract. Spread over crust.

Bake at 375° for 45 minutes.

Icing
1 cup powdered sugar, sifted
1½ tablespoons cream
1 tablespoon butter, softened
2 teaspoons almond extract

Beat icing ingredients. Spread on top of cake. Sprinkle with sliced almonds.

Banana Muffins

These moist muffins are worth the effort!
Make in advance, and take them along. They freeze well.

2 cups sugar

½ cup shortening

2 tablespoons vegetable oil

2 cups mashed bananas

3 eggs

2¼ cups cake flour

2½ teaspoons baking soda

2½ teaspoons baking powder

¾ teaspoon salt

¾ teaspoon vanilla

1½ teaspoons lemon juice

1 cup buttermilk

Cream sugar, shortening and oil. Add bananas and cream well. Add eggs and mix well. Combine dry ingredients and add to first mixture. Add vanilla and lemon juice. Mix well at low speed. Gradually add buttermilk until smooth. Mix at medium speed for 3 minutes. Put into greased or paper-lined muffin pans

Bake at 380° for 20 to 22 minutes.

Makes about 2 dozen muffins.

Big Pine French Toast

2 cups milk

4 eggs, well beaten

½ teaspoon salt

2 teaspoons cinnamon (optional)

Bread

Mix all ingredients. Dip bread into mixture until well coated.

Fry on oiled griddle or fry pan until golden brown.

Makes 24.

Blueberry Muffins

Freezes well.

½ cup margarine
1½ cups sugar
2 eggs
½ cup milk
½ teaspoon salt
2 teaspoons baking powder
2 cups flour
2½ cups (1 pint) frozen or
   fresh blueberries

Using a spoon, mix all ingredients except blueberries. (Do not use a mixer.) Fold blueberries into batter. Line muffin tins with paper cups. Fill to top of paper liner. Sprinkle each muffin with a teaspoon of sugar.

Bake at 375° for 25 to 30 minutes.

Makes 16 muffins.

Breakfast Muffins

⅓ cup margarine
½ cup sugar
1 egg
1½ cups flour
1½ teaspoons baking powder
½ teaspoon salt
¼ teaspoon nutmeg
½ cup milk

½ cup sugar
1 teaspoon cinnamon
½ cup butter, melted

Combine and mix margarine, sugar and egg. In another bowl, combine flour, baking powder, salt and nutmeg. Add dry mixture, alternately with milk, to first mixture. Fill greased muffin cups ⅔ full.

Bake at 350° for 20 to 25 minutes.

Mix sugar and cinnamon. Immediately after baking, roll hot muffins in melted butter, then in sugar. Serve hot.

Makes 12 muffins.

Bran Muffins

Batter can be stored in refrigerator up to 6 weeks.
A good fiber food to have on hand for those who love to drop in!

1 15-ounce package
  Raisin Bran
5 cups flour
5 teaspoons baking soda
2 teaspoons salt
3 cups sugar
½ cup vegetable oil
½ cup butter, melted
1 quart buttermilk, at room
  temperature
4 eggs, lightly beaten
1 cup nuts, chopped
1 cup raisins or dates

Melt butter. Let cool. In a 4-quart bowl, combine cereal, flour, baking soda, salt and sugar. Mix oil, butter, buttermilk, eggs, nuts and raisins. Stir into dry ingredients. Cover lightly. Store in refrigerator. Use as needed. Fill greased muffin cups ⅔ full with batter.

Bake at 350° for 20 minutes.

Makes 6 dozen muffins.

Pumpkin Raisin Muffins

Freezes very well.

1 30-ounce can pumpkin
  pie mix
2 16.1-ounce packages nut
  bread mix
1 egg, beaten
1 cup raisins
2 tablespoons sugar
1 teaspoon cinnamon

Heat oven to 375°. Combine pumpkin pie mix, nut bread mix and egg. Mix only until bread mix is moistened. Stir in raisins. Fill greased muffin cups or paper muffin cups ⅔ full of batter. Combine sugar and cinnamon. Sprinkle on top of muffins.

Bake 15 to 20 minutes, or until golden brown.

Makes 30 muffins.

Toasty Nut Granola

This is a popular, nutritious and filling breakfast cereal for the late-rising college crowd. It tides them over until noon without messing up the kitchen!

6 cups oatmeal, uncooked
½ cup brown sugar
¾ cup wheat germ
½ cup coconut
⅓ cup sesame seeds
1 cup chopped nuts
½ cup vegetable oil
⅓ cup honey
1½ teaspoons vanilla

Heat oatmeal at 350° in ungreased 9-by-13-inch pan for 10 minutes. Mix brown sugar, wheat germ, coconut, sesame seeds and chopped nuts into heated oatmeal.

Combine vegetable oil, honey and vanilla. Add to first mixture, coating dry ingredients. Divide mixture into two equal parts, putting each in a 9-by-13-inch pan (or bake one pan at a time).

Bake for 20 minutes, stirring often to brown evenly. Cool. Store in tightly covered container. Add raisins, if desired.

Serve with milk and fresh fruit, if desired. This may also be used as a topping for vanilla ice cream.

Apple-Oatmeal Baked Breakfast

A delicious way to "take the chill off" on a crisp morning!

2 cups milk

2 tablespoons brown sugar

1 tablespoon butter

¼ teaspoon salt

¼ teaspoon cinnamon

1 cup rolled oats

1 cup apples, peeled and diced

½ cup raisins

Combine milk, brown sugar, butter, salt and cinnamon in a pan. Scald. Add oats, apples and raisins. Heat until bubbles appear at edge of saucepan. Put into greased 1½-quart casserole.

Bake at 350° for 30 minutes. After 15 minutes of baking, stir in 1 tablespoon of brown sugar. Serve with milk or cream.

Serves 4 to 6.

Puffy French Toast

1 cup flour, sifted

1½ teaspoon sugar

1½ teaspoons baking powder

½ teaspoon salt

¼ teaspoon cinnamon

1 cup milk

1 egg, beaten

8 slices white bread

Oil for deep frying

Sift dry ingredients. Blend milk and egg. Add to flour mixture. Beat until smooth. Dip bread slices into batter, turning to coat both sides evenly.

Fry in preheated deep oil (375°) until golden brown, about 2 minutes on each side. Drain. Serve hot.

Makes 8 slices.

Frozen Orange French Toast

2 eggs
1 cup orange juice
1 tablespoon sugar
¼ teaspoon salt
12 slices French bread
6 tablespoons butter or
  margarine

Advance preparation: Beat first 4 ingredients. Dip bread into egg mixture, coating both sides. Place bread on baking sheets. Freeze until firm. Wrap. Return to freezer.

Before serving: Place bread slices in well-buttered, shallow baking pan. Melt butter, and drizzle over bread.

Bake in 500° oven for 5 minutes. Turn over, and bake about 5 minutes more. Serve with syrup and butter, if desired.

Serves 6.

Hootenanny Pancakes

½ cup margarine or butter
6 eggs
1 cup milk
1 cup flour
½ teaspoon salt

Melt butter in 9-by-13-inch glass pan in 425° oven. Beat eggs and milk. Add flour and salt. Do not overbeat. Pour into pan.

Bake for 25 to 30 minutes. Serve with syrup, jam, jelly, powdered sugar, cinnamon sugar or thinly sliced apples.

Serves 6.

Make-Ahead Pancake Mix

Store in a covered container. Handy!

10 cups flour

2 cups powdered milk

6 tablespoons baking powder

1½ tablespoons salt

1½ teaspoons cream of tartar

¼ cup sugar

2 cups shortening

Sift dry ingredients 3 times. Cut shortening into dry mixture. Store in covered container.

Beat milk and egg. Add mix.

Cook on hot griddle.

Pancakes for 4

1 cup milk

1 egg

1½ cups pancake mix

Crisp Waffles

This recipe is especially good for thick waffles similar to those cooked in a Belgian waffle iron.

2 eggs, separated

1 cup flour

1 cup milk

½ teaspoon salt

1 teaspoon sugar

2 tablespoons vegetable oil

2 tablespoons melted butter

4 teaspoons baking powder

Mix egg yolks, flour, milk, salt, sugar, oil and melted butter. Beat egg whites until stiff, but not dry. Add to first mixture. Just before baking, fold in baking powder.

Bake in preheated waffle iron.

Makes 4 waffles, depending on size of waffle iron.

German Pancake
Bring to the table in the skillet—attractive!

4 tablespoons (½ stick) butter

1 cup flour

1 cup milk

4 eggs

Dash of salt

Heat oven to 425°. Melt butter in a 10-inch cast iron skillet in oven. Add remaining ingredients to melted butter. Stir for 45 seconds. Batter will remain somewhat lumpy.

Bake at 425° for 12 to 15 minutes. Sprinkle with powdered sugar, if you wish. Serve with sausage or bacon. Top with jam, syrup, warm applesauce, or sour cream and fresh fruit or berries.

Serves 4.

Finnish Oven Pancakes

This easy breakfast just might become a favorite.

4 eggs

4 cups milk

2 cups flour

¼ teaspoon salt

1 teaspoon sugar

Preheat oven to 450°. Mix all ingredients. In each of two 9-by-13-inch pans, melt 1 tablespoon of butter in preheating oven. Remove pans from oven when butter is melted. Divide ingredients into the 2 pans

Bake at 450° for about 15 minutes, or until crispy brown on edges and golden and bubbly on top. Serve at once with syrup or jam.

Serves 6.

Egg & Cheese Dishes

Egg and Cheese Brunch

Put this together 24 hours before it will be served.

8 slices bread, crusts removed, cubed

1 pound sharp cheddar cheese, grated

1 cup diced ham

6 eggs

1½ cups half-and-half

½ teaspoon dry mustard

½ teaspoon salt

Butter a 9-by-13-inch pan. Put bread cubes in bottom of pan. Cover with cheese and ham. Combine eggs, half-and-half, dry mustard and salt. Pour over bread and cheese.

Cover and refrigerate for 24 hours. Remove from refrigerator 2 hours before baking.

Bake, uncovered, at 325° for 1½ hours.

Serves 8.

Company-at-the-Cabin Brunch

18 eggs

1 cup plus 2 tablespoons half-and-half

3 tablespoons butter

1 10½-ounce can mushroom soup

6-ounce can mushrooms, drained

5 ounces (about 1¼ cups) shredded cheddar cheese

3 to 4 slices bacon, crisply fried and crumbled

Combine eggs and half-and-half. Beat. Scramble lightly in butter in large skillet. Put eggs in large, shallow casserole or pan. Pour on soup, mushrooms and cheese. Top with bacon.

Bake at 250° for 45 to 60 minutes. This can be made the night before and refrigerated before baking. If so, bake 1½ hours.

Serves 10 to 12.

Lazy Day Supper, for Two

4 eggs

½ cup (or more) cheddar
cheese, grated

¼ cup (scant) whipping cream

Butter a small casserole.
Sprinkle half of the cheese on
bottom of casserole. Put eggs
on cheese, as you would for
fried eggs. (Line up the eggs so
it will be easy to cut after baking.) Sprinkle remaining cheese
over eggs. Salt and pepper to
taste. Pour cream over all.

Bake, uncovered, at 350° for
15 to 20 minutes, or until
center is no longer runny
when you shake the casserole.

This recipe can easily be doubled. It can also be quadrupled
in a 9-by-13-inch pan, baking
for 30 to 40 minutes.

Serves 2.

Super Simple Supper
Serve with toast and fresh fruit for a quick meal.

4 slices bacon, cut up

1 can (1 pound) cream style
corn, drained

5 eggs, lightly beaten

Seasoned salt

Sauté and drain bacon pieces.
Add well-drained corn.
Simmer until warm.

Add eggs and stir, as for
scrambled eggs. Sprinkle to
taste with seasoned salt.

Serves 4.

Lake Country Eggs and Sausage
Prepare the night before.

4 slices white bread, cubed

1 cup shredded sharp cheese

¾ pound bulk sausage, cooked and drained

4 eggs, beaten

1¼ cups milk

¼ teaspoon dry mustard

Half of a 10½-ounce can mushroom soup

¼ cup milk

Layer bread, cheese and sausage in a greased 8-by-8-inch pan or casserole. Combine eggs, 1¼ cups milk and dry mustard; pour over all.

Cover and refrigerate overnight. Just before popping in the oven, combine soup and ¼ cup milk. Pour over top of casserole.

Bake, uncovered, at 300° for 1½ hours. A double recipe can be made in a 9-by-13-inch pan.

Serves 4.

Fluffy Oven Eggs and Bacon

½ pound bacon
(about 12 slices)

½ cup chopped onion

½ cup Bisquick

3 eggs

1¼ cups milk

¼ teaspoon salt

⅛ teaspoon pepper

½ cup shredded cheddar or
Swiss cheese

Grease 1½-quart round casserole. Cut bacon slices into thirds Cook and stir bacon in 10-inch skillet over medium heat, until almost crisp. Add onion. Cook, stirring frequently, until bacon is crisp. Drain. Spread bacon and onion in bottom of casserole.

Beat Bisquick, eggs, milk, salt and pepper with hand beater, until almost smooth. Slowly pour egg mixture over bacon; sprinkle with cheese.

Bake in 375° oven, uncovered, until knife inserted in center comes out clean, about 35 minutes.

Serves 4 to 6.

Impossible Quiche

Before you take off for the lake, mix butter, milk, Bisquick, eggs and seasonings in a quart jar. Fry the bacon, and crumble into pieces. Chop and sauté the onion. Shred the cheese. Place in separate baggies. When you arrive at your cabin, just combine the ingredients and this special supper is ready in 1 hour.

6 tablespoons butter, melted

12 slices bacon, diced, or
1 cup cooked ham, diced

⅓ cup finely chopped onion

1½ cups (6 ounces) shredded Swiss or cheddar cheese

1 4-ounce can sliced mushrooms (optional)

1½ cups milk

½ cup Bisquick

3 eggs

¼ teaspoon salt

⅛ teaspoon pepper

Lightly grease a 10-inch pie plate. Fry bacon until crisp and crumble into pan. Sauté onion in bacon grease. Sprinkle onion, cheese and mushrooms evenly over bacon. In blender, mix remaining ingredients on high speed for 1 minute, or use hand mixer. Pour into pie plate.

Bake at 350° for 50 to 60 minutes, until golden, and knife comes out clean when inserted in center of quiche. Let stand for 5 minutes before cutting.

Serves 6 to 8.

Cottage Cheese Spinach Quiche

No crust needed!

1 cup cottage cheese

10 ounces frozen chopped
spinach, well drained
(squeezed)

3 eggs, beaten

1 scant teaspoon Lawry's
seasoned salt

Sprinkling of nutmeg

½ cup Parmesan cheese

Paprika

Mix all ingredients, except the paprika. Pour into buttered 9-inch pie plate. Sprinkle with paprika.

Bake at 350° for 30 minutes.

Serves 6.

Shrimp Pie

Good for Sunday brunch.
Serve with a fresh fruit cup and bran muffins.

1 8-ounce can crescent rolls

1½ cups shredded
cheddar cheese, divided

3 eggs

1 10½-ounce can cream of
shrimp soup

¼ cup chopped celery

¼ cup chopped green pepper

2 tablespoons chopped onion

Salt

Pepper

Spread out roll dough in un-greased 9-by-13-inch baking dish. Press over bottom of dish and ½ inch up sides to form crust. Sprinkle 1 cup cheese over crust. Beat eggs. Add soup, celery, green pepper, onion, salt and pepper. Pour over cheese and crust. Sprinkle with remaining cheese.

Bake, uncovered, at 375° for 30 to 35 minutes, or until knife inserted off-center comes out clean.

Serves 6 to 8.

Broccoli Soufflé

4 tablespoons butter
½ cup chopped onion
2 tablespoons flour
½ teaspoon salt
½ cup water
8-ounce jar Cheez Whiz
3 eggs, beaten
2 10-ounce packages frozen
  chopped broccoli
Cracker crumbs

Sauté butter and onions in pan. Add flour, salt and water. Stir until thick. Add Cheez Whiz. Stir, and let stand.

Mix cooked and drained broccoli with beaten eggs. Pour into cheese mixture. Put into 1½-quart greased casserole. Sprinkle with cracker crumbs.

Bake, uncovered, at 325° for 45 minutes.

Serves 6 to 8.

Gruyere Oven Omelet

This recipe can easily be cut in half.

8 eggs
1 cup milk
¼ pound Canadian bacon,
  or ham, cut up
2½ cups (10 ounces)
  shredded Gruyere cheese
⅛ teaspoon nutmeg
Sprinkling of salt
Sprinkling of pepper
1 tablespoon melted butter

Beat eggs. Add remaining ingredients, except butter. Pour into buttered 2-quart baking dish. Drizzle top with butter.

Bake, uncovered, at 350° for 40 minutes.

Serves 6 to 8.

Eggs Albuquerque

Can be made in advance and stored in the refrigerator.

1 pint cottage cheese

½ cup butter or margarine, melted

½ cup flour

Dash of salt

1 pound Monterey Jack cheese, shredded

10 large eggs

1 teaspoon baking powder

1 8-ounce can chopped green chilies, rinsed and drained

Melt butter. Beat eggs lightly in large bowl. Blend in flour, baking powder and salt. Add melted butter, chilies, cottage cheese and Monterey Jack cheese.

Bake, uncovered, in 9-by-13-inch baking pan at 400° for 15 minutes and at 350° for 35 to 40 minutes. Cut into squares while warm.

Serves 8 to 10.

Poached Eggs Supreme

A good breakfast when people get up at different times.

1 egg

1 strip bacon

1 piece of toast

1 slice American cheese

Poach egg in water for 4 minutes. Fry bacon. Top buttered toast with cheese, bacon and the poached egg.

Broil for 1 minute, or until cheese starts to melt. Must be eaten immediately.

Ham 'n' Eggs

A tasty choice for a birthday brunch.

1 6-ounce box shredded
   hash browns

1 6½-ounce can chopped ham

1 cup shredded cheddar
   cheese

6 eggs, beaten

1 cup milk

Soak hash browns in water until they soften. Drain. Pat into a 9-by-9-inch pan. Layer ham and cheese. Add green pepper or onions, if you desire. Mix eggs and milk. Pour into pan.

Bake at 350° for 45 to 60 minutes.

Serves 4.

Ham and Egg Pizza

1 tube refrigerated
   crescent rolls

¼ cup chopped onion

¼ cup butter

1 cup chopped ham
   (or bacon or turkey)

4 eggs

½ cup milk

Salt and pepper

1 cup shredded cheese
   (Swiss or Monterey Jack)

Spread rolls onto pizza pan to make crust. Sauté onion in butter. Add ham. Pour over crust.

Combine and beat the eggs, milk, salt and pepper. Pour over ham and onion. Sprinkle cheese on top.

Bake at 350° for 30 minutes, or until brown.

Makes 1 pizza.

Soups & Sandwiches

Overnite Barbecue Beef Sandwiches

This is great for a crowd at the lake. Guests can help
themselves when they are hungry.
Caution: Make plenty, or the last ones may find an empty pot.

4–5 pound boneless pork
or beef roast

½ cup water

1 onion, sliced or chopped

1 16-ounce bottle
barbecue sauce

Buns or French bread

Cook roast with water in crock pot on low heat for 10 to 12 hours. Remove. Slice thin. Return to crock pot. Add onion and barbecue sauce.

Cook on low for another 4 to 6 hours. Serve on buns or French bread.

Self-Serve Sandwich

1 loaf French bread

Lunch meat, sliced

Cheese, sliced

Lettuce

Tomato, sliced

Onion, sliced (optional)

Cut bread lengthwise. Butter bottom; put mayonnaise on top. Layer meat, cheese, tomato and onion. Top with lettuce. Replace top of bread. Slide back into bread wrapper.

As hunger pangs hit, the loaf can be pulled out, the desired amount sliced off, and the rest returned to the wrapper.

Hot Ham and Cheese Sandwiches

The key to this super sandwich is the spread. These sandwiches can be prepared in advance and refrigerated or frozen before baking. Good with potato salad.

½ cup (1 stick) butter or margarine

2 tablespoons prepared mustard

1 tablespoon poppy seed

½ tablespoon Worcestershire sauce

2 tablespoons minced onion

6 sandwich rolls or rye buns

Sliced ham

6 slices Swiss cheese

Combine first 5 ingredients. Open rolls or buns. Spread mixture on top and bottom, as for sandwich. Place ham and cheese in roll. Wrap individually in foil.

Bake at 350° for 15 minutes. Serve immediately. If frozen, thaw before baking.

For appetizers, use Pepperidge Farm Party Rolls. Without separating rolls, slice in half horizontally. Spread with butter mixture. Put ham and cheese on roll slices. Cut into individual servings, either before or after baking.

Spamwiches

This mixture can be made ahead and kept in the refrigerator, then used as a spread, hot or cold.

1 can Spam, cut up

¼ cup processed cheese, cut up

1 small onion, cut up

1–2 dill pickles, cut up

¾ cup mayonnaise

Blend all ingredients in blender or food processor. Spread on hot dog buns. Wrap individual buns in foil. Warm in 350° oven for about 15 minutes.

Tuna-Cheese Melt

1 6 ½-ounce can tuna, drained

2 tablespoons finely
  chopped onion

2 tablespoons diced celery

2 tablespoons mayonnaise or
  salad dressing

¼ teaspoon salt

¼ teaspoon pepper

2 English muffins, split

4 slices tomato

4 slices cheese (Swiss or
  processed American)

Combine first 6 ingredients.
Toast and butter the muffin
halves. Layer on each: ¼ of the
tuna mixture, a tomato slice
and a slice of cheese.

Bake, uncovered, at 350° for
5 to 7 minutes, or until cheese
is melted.

Serves 4.

Stovetop Hot Beef for Sandwiches
This keeps well for later reheating.

1 chuck roast

Beef bouillon cubes or
  instant granules

1 package dry onion soup mix

1 cup tomato juice

Brown roast over low heat.
Add water to cover. Add
bouillon—1 cube or
1 teaspoon for each cup
of water used.

Simmer for 3 to 5 hours
or until most of liquid is
absorbed and meat can be
easily shredded. Shred meat.
Add soup mix and juice.
Reheat. Serve on buns.

Minnetonka Steak Sandwich

A super-fast meal—try it with fresh sweet corn!

3 breakfast steaks (sirloin tip, sliced very thin)

French or sourdough bread

Dip

½ cup butter

3 tablespoons Heinz 57 sauce

2 tablespoons sliced green onion

In saucepan, combine butter, sauce and green onion. Cook on low, until butter is melted and onion is soft.

In hot fry pan, grill steaks for about 3 minutes (1½ minutes on each side). Dip bread and steak into sauce before making open-faced sandwich.

Serves 3.

Tuna-Filled Buns

Make the filling at home, and take it with you.

¼ pound cubed or shredded cheddar cheese

3 hard-cooked eggs, diced

1 can tuna

2 tablespoons diced green pepper (optional)

2 tablespoons diced stuffed olives (optional)

2 tablespoons diced sweet pickles (optional)

½ cup mayonnaise

6 buns

Combine all ingredients, except buns. Mix well. Place in 6 buns, and wrap each in foil.

Bake at 250° for 30 minutes.

Filling is best when made the day before.

Relaxed Roast Beef Sandwiches

Fantastic for several meals at the cabin.

**4-pound rolled,
  or rump, roast**

Vegetable oil

3 beef bouillon cubes

2 cups boiling water

1 package dry onion soup

Brown beef roast in oil on all sides. Dissolve bouillon in water. Add onion soup. Pour over roast.

Roast in covered pan at 250° for about 3 hours, depending upon what doneness you desire. Cool meat. Slice thin. Put back into juice. (Be sure juice covers meat; add water, if necessary.) Let meat marinate at least a day. May be made 3 or 4 days ahead of time and marinated in refrigerator, or may be frozen.

When ready to use, heat slowly on top of stove. Serve as an open-faced sandwich, with sauce on the side.

Serves 10 to 12.

Hot Dog Toasties

8 wieners

8 slices of bread

Soft butter or margarine

Mustard, if desired

8 slices American cheese

¼ cup butter or margarine,
  melted

Drop wieners into boiling water. Reduce heat. Cover, and simmer for 5 to 8 minutes.

Spread bread with soft butter and mustard. Place bread on cookie sheet or broiler pan. Top each bread slice with a slice of cheese. Place wieners diagonally on cheese. Fold bread over to form a triangle, and secure with toothpicks. Brush with melted butter.

Broil 3 to 4 inches from heat for about 2 minutes, or until golden brown.

Serves 8.

Spread for Open-Faced Burger

1 pound hamburger

1 teaspoon
  Worcestershire sauce

1 teaspoon oregano

Salt and pepper to taste

1 cup shredded cheddar or
  American cheese

Mix all ingredients. Spread rather thinly on half of a hamburger bun or English muffin.

Bake at 300° for 15 to 20 minutes. Watch carefully.

Makes 16 half-bun servings.

Baked Souper Sandwich

1½ pounds ground beef

1 small onion, chopped

½ cup chopped celery

½ teaspoon salt

4 cups herb-seasoned stuffing cubes

1½ cups milk

2 eggs

1 10½-ounce can cream of mushroom soup

1 teaspoon dry mustard

1 cup shredded cheddar cheese

Brown the meat, onion and celery. Drain. Mix in salt. Put stuffing cubes in greased baking pan, 9-by-9-inch or 12-by-8-inch. Top with meat. Beat milk, eggs, soup and mustard. Pour over meat. Sprinkle with cheese.

Bake at 350°, uncovered, for 30 to 40 minutes, or until knife inserted in center comes out clean. Cool for 5 minutes, and cut into squares.

Serves 6.

Sloppy Joes

We send this along with our hunters for a filling supper after the shoot.

1 pound ground beef

1 package French's sloppy joe mix

1 6-ounce can tomato paste

1 10½-ounce can chicken rice soup

1 can water

Brown hamburger. Drain fat. Add sloppy joe mix, tomato paste, soup and water.

Simmer for ½ hour. Serve on buns, toasted if desired.

Easiest Sloppy Joes

Or ... how come I never heard of this before?

1–1½ pounds ground beef

Chopped onion (optional)

1 12-ounce bottle chili sauce

Brown ground beef and onion. No seasonings necessary. Drain fat. Add chili sauce and heat thoroughly.

Fills 4 to 6 buns.

Sloppy Josephs

1 pound hamburger

½ cup chopped onion

1 10½-ounce can chicken gumbo soup

3 tablespoons ketchup, minimum

1–2 tablespoons prepared mustard

Brown hamburger and onion. Drain fat. Mix all ingredients.

Simmer for 30 minutes.

Fills 8 hamburger buns.

Easy Pizzas

1 package English muffins, halved

1 jar pizza sauce or spaghetti sauce

1 package sliced pepperoni

1 package shredded mozzarella cheese

Place muffin halves on cookie sheet. Spread with pizza sauce. Divide pepperoni among the muffins, covering the pizza sauce. Sprinkle cheese on top.

Bake at 300° for 15 to 20 minutes.

Open-Faced Hamburgers

*A good way to use up miscellaneous buns, bread, English muffins, etc.
It's also a real meat stretcher!*

½ **pound ground beef**

1 **small onion, chopped**

2–3 **tablespoons milk**

½ **teaspoon salt**

Sprinkle of pepper

Bread or buns

Combine first 5 ingredients. Spread on buttered bread or bun halves, all the way to the edges. (You can also first toast the bread or buns on the bottom side under a broiler.)

Broil until browned. Serve with mustard or ketchup. Easy to make in multiples.

Covers 4 bread or bun pieces.

Hamburger Goo

A favorite from a Lake Superior-cabin family.

6 **slices bacon, chopped**

1 **small onion, chopped**

1 **pound hamburger**

1 **10½-ounce can tomato soup**

1 **cup cubed Velveeta cheese**

Hamburger buns

Sauté bacon and onion. Add hamburger and brown. Drain fat. Add soup. Cool. Add cheese. Spread on halves of hamburger buns for open–faced sandwiches.

Bake at 350° for 15 to 20 minutes.

Fills 16 to 20 bun halves.

Larry's Juicy Hamburgers

These patties can be mixed, shaped and frozen for later use.

2 pounds hamburger
½ cup grated apple
½ teaspoon salt
¼ teaspoon black pepper
¼ teaspoon Italian seasoning
2 eggs, beaten
½ cup cracker crumbs

Combine and blend all ingredients.

Fry or broil to desired doneness. Serve on buns.

Makes 10 patties.

Hearty Hamburger Soup

So good on a "fall-is-near" evening. Keeps for days in the refrigerator. Freezes well.

1½ pounds hamburger,
    browned and drained
1 small onion, chopped
4 carrots, chopped
2 stalks celery, chopped
    (use tops, too)
2 10½-ounce cans
    beef consommé
2 soup cans water
½ cup barley
1 28-ounce can tomatoes
1 teaspoon salt
¼ teaspoon pepper
¼ teaspoon thyme
1 bay leaf

Sauté onion lightly in butter. Brown hamburger. Drain fat. Combine all ingredients.

Simmer for 1 hour.

Serves at least 8.

Uncle Ole's Clam-Shrimp Chowder

This thick Manhattan-style chowder is a favorite of a group of men who hunt and fish together.

12 slices bacon, cut into ½-inch squares

1 cup chopped onions

1 cup grated carrots

1 cup chopped celery

1 green pepper, finely chopped

4 cups milk

6 10½-ounce cans potato soup

3 10½-ounce cans tomato bisque soup

5 7-ounce cans minced clams (do not drain; use juice, too)

2 7-ounce cans small whole shrimp, drained

1 small jar pimento, cut up

Seasonings
Morton's seasoning blend, Lawry's seasoned salt, parsley, oregano, pepper, etc.

1 cup dry vermouth or wine (optional)

Fry bacon until crisp. Sauté onions, carrots, celery and green pepper until tender. Drain grease.

In a large kettle, combine milk, soups, clams and juice, shrimp and pimento. Simmer, stirring occasionally. Add bacon and vegetables. Season to your own taste. Add vermouth, if desired.

Makes 5 quarts—12 hearty servings.

Navy Bean Soup

Good with crackers or cornbread. Freezes well.

1 pound navy beans
1 teaspoon baking soda
1 ham hock with meat on it
(or ham leftovers, diced)
2 potatoes, peeled and diced
1 medium onion, diced
1½ teaspoons salt

Cover beans with water (1 inch above bean level). Add baking soda. Soak for at least 8 hours.

Drain beans, and add ham hock, potatoes, onion and salt. Barely cover all with water. Cover, and bring to a slow boil. Cook until beans are tender, about 5 hours. Remove bone after ham falls off.

Serves 8.

Meat Ball Soup

1 pound hamburger
1 tablespoon minced onion
1 egg, beaten
½ cup bread crumbs
¼ teaspoon salt
¼ teaspoon pepper
1 16-ounce can stewed
tomatoes
1 8-ounce can tomato sauce
1 8-ounce can mixed
vegetables
1 tablespoon sugar
1 cup water
1 envelope French onion
soup mix

Combine hamburger, onion, egg, bread crumbs, salt and pepper. Shape into small balls. Brown in oil. Place remaining ingredients in a large kettle.

Heat to boiling. Add meatballs. Simmer, covered, for 15 minutes.

Serves 6 to 8.

Gazpacho

A fine cold soup. Serve with nachos or toast for lunch, or as a first course.

1 cucumber, peeled, seeded, finely diced

3 tomatoes, peeled, seeded, diced

1 green pepper, diced

1 small can black olives, chopped

1 clove garlic, finely diced (or ¼ teaspoon garlic powder)

3 stalks celery, diced

2 teaspoons vinegar

¼ teaspoon salt

¼ cup vegetable oil

1 tablespoon snipped parsley

2 teaspoons minced green onions

2 tablespoons lemon juice

Combine cucumber, tomatoes, green pepper, olives, garlic and celery. Combine vinegar, salt, oil, parsley and onions, and mix with vegetables. Pour lemon juice over mixture.

Refrigerate for several hours to blend flavors. Serve in cold bowls or cups. Can garnish with a dollop of sour cream. Keeps for several days in the refrigerator.

Serves 8.

Salads & Dressings

Pasta Vegetable Salad
Very tasty!

1 7-ounce package
macaroni rings
2 cups finely chopped cabbage
½ cup finely diced cucumber
½ cup finely diced
green pepper
1 tablespoon finely
diced onion
½ cup sugar
¼ cup vinegar
1 cup Miracle Whip dressing

Prepare macaroni according to package directions. Drain. Add vegetables. Combine sugar, vinegar and Miracle Whip. Pour over macaroni and vegetables.

Refrigerate in 3-quart container. Keeps well in cooler or refrigerator.

Serves 8.

Fresh Veggie Salad
Good for a "potluck" at the lake. Make the day before you'll need it.

1 head cauliflower
1 bunch broccoli
1 large green pepper, chopped
1 sweet red onion,
separated into rings
1 box cherry tomatoes
1 can sliced water chestnuts
1 can pitted ripe olives
2 envelopes Good Seasons
Italian salad dressing mix

Cut vegetables into bite-sized pieces. Mix salad dressing until creamy, according to package instructions, adding extra tablespoon of oil. Add dressing to vegetables. Toss well. Marinate overnight.

Variations: ½ pound sliced fresh mushrooms, and sliced celery. Half of the recipe will serve 4 to 6 for a main course. Good with popovers!

Serves 12 to 14.

Pea Salad
Good to prepare ahead of time—travels well.

1 10-ounce package
  frozen peas
½ cup diced cheddar cheese
2 hard-cooked eggs, sliced
¼ cup chopped celery
2 tablespoons chopped onion
3 tomatoes, chopped
⅓ cup mayonnaise
½ teaspoon salt
⅛ teaspoon pepper
¼ teaspoon Tabasco sauce

Mix first 6 ingredients. Combine mayonnaise, salt, pepper and Tabasco. Toss and chill. Keep refrigerated.

Serves 6.

Tasty Marinated Vegetable Salad
Make ahead of time and refrigerate or freeze.

1 16-ounce can green beans
1 16-ounce can wax beans
1 16-ounce can small
  whole carrots
8 ounces button (whole)
  mushrooms
1 small jar pimento
1 onion, finely chopped

Marinade
½ cup vegetable oil
1½ cups sugar
1 cup vinegar
1 teaspoon salt
1 teaspoon celery seed
½ teaspoon paprika
Sprinkle of garlic salt

Drain vegetables. Mix together. Mix marinade. Pour over vegetables.

Let stand about 12 hours in refrigerator, stirring occasionally. At this point it may be frozen, or it will keep in refrigerator for several days.

Serves 10.

Spinach Salad

1 pound fresh spinach, washed and drained

Small container of bean sprouts

¼ pound fresh mushrooms, sliced

1 onion, sliced and separated into rings

1 8-ounce can water chestnuts, drained and sliced

½ pound bacon, fried and broken into pieces

Dressing
1 cup vegetable oil

¼ cup vinegar

½ cup sugar

1 tablespoon Worcestershire sauce

1 medium onion, grated

⅓ cup ketchup

½ teaspoon salt

Combine spinach, bean sprouts, mushrooms, onion, water chestnuts and bacon.

Mix dressing in 1-quart jar. Shake well. Sprinkle over vegetables. Toss.

Soupy Salad
Grandpa's favorite luncheon dish. Low in sugar and salt.

2 carrots, shredded

1 celery stalk, chopped

1 medium tomato, sliced

Cucumber slices

Mayonnaise

Applesauce, natural

Yogurt, plain or vanilla

Cheese, shredded

Coconut

Place carrots, celery, tomato and cucumber in bowl. Mix mayonnaise, applesauce and yogurt. Pour over vegetables. Stir lightly. Garnish with cheese and coconut. Serve with hard-boiled eggs and wheat crackers.

Overnight Layered Salad

1 head lettuce, finely chopped

½ cup chopped green onion

1 cup chopped celery
(2 medium stalks)

1 4½-ounce can water chestnuts, drained and sliced

10 ounces uncooked
frozen peas, drained

2 medium tomatoes, diced

Place lettuce in a 9-by-13-inch pan. Layer with remaining salad ingredients.

Dressing

2 cups mayonnaise

1 teaspoon seasoned salt

¼ teaspoon garlic powder

Combine dressing ingredients. Spread over salad.

Topping

½ pound cooked bacon,
diced, or ¾ to 1 cup bacon-
flavored protein pieces

3 hard-cooked eggs, chopped

Parmesan cheese

Top dressing with bacon, eggs and Parmesan cheese. Refrigerate overnight.

Serves 10 to 12.

Summer Salad
Colorful and crunchy.

10 radishes, chopped

2 cups chopped broccoli

3 cups chopped cauliflower

½ cup chopped celery

4–6 green onions (tops, too)

3–4 carrots, sliced into
coin shape

½ cup chopped green pepper

Cherry tomatoes

Cucumbers

Dressing

1 cup sour cream

½ cup mayonnaise

½ package Good Seasons
Cheese and Garlic dressing

Mix dressing and vegetables
20 minutes before serving.

Fresh Broccoli Salad

1 pound fresh broccoli, cut
into bite-sized pieces

2 tablespoons chopped
green onions

2 large tomatoes, chopped

Dressing

½ cup mayonnaise

1 tablespoon lemon juice

½ teaspoon salt

¼ teaspoon pepper

Cook broccoli. Chill. Toss with
dressing just before serving.

Marinated Carrots

A tasty cold carrot salad or accompaniment that can be done a day or two before you'll need it.

2 pounds carrots

1 large onion, thinly sliced

1 large green pepper, cut into thin strips

1 can tomato soup

1 cup sugar

½ cup vegetable oil

¾ cup vinegar

1 teaspoon salt

½ teaspoon pepper

¼ teaspoon dill weed

Peel, slice and cook carrots until just tender. Drain and cool. Put carrots, onion and green pepper in 2-quart bowl or jar. Mix together in a saucepan, the soup and all ingredients following it. Bring to a boil. Stir. Pour hot soup mixture over vegetables. Cover.

Refrigerate. Make at least 12 hours before serving. It keeps well for several days.

Serves 10.

Carrot-Tuna-Shoestring Salad

An unusual combination of ingredients that is excellent.

6 carrots, grated

1 can tuna, drained

½ cup diced celery

1 small onion, chopped

1 cup mayonnaise

2 tablespoons French dressing

2 tablespoons sugar

1 cup (or more) shoestring potatoes

Mix carrots, tuna, celery and onion. Mix mayonnaise, French dressing and sugar. Toss with vegetables.

Chill for a few hours before serving. Just before serving, stir in shoestring potatoes.

Serves 6.

Three-Bean Salad

Almost everyone makes this and likes it.
We include it in case you forgot how to make the dressing!

1 can green beans, drained

1 can wax beans, drained

1 can kidney beans, drained

1 small green pepper, chopped

1 cup sliced celery

½ cup chopped onion

1 jar button mushrooms

½ cup vegetable oil

¾ cup sugar

⅔ cup vinegar

½ teaspoon salt

½ teaspoon pepper

Combine vegetables. Combine oil, sugar, vinegar, salt and pepper. Pour over vegetables.

Marinate overnight before serving. Travels well and keeps for days. For lunch, serve on a bed of shredded lettuce, with toast.

Serves 10 to 12.

Calypso Salad

1 12-ounce can
 mexicorn, drained

4 cups shredded cabbage

¼ cup finely chopped onion

¼ cup cubed sharp
 cheddar cheese

¼ cup sliced black olives

Dressing
1 cup mayonnaise

2 tablespoons white vinegar

2 tablespoons sugar

1 tablespoon prepared mustard

¼ teaspoon celery seed

Salt to taste

Combine dressing ingredients. Mix well with other ingredients. Let stand ½ hour before serving.

Serves 8 to 10.

Mexican Chip Salad
It's crunchy, tasty and filling!

2 pounds ground beef
1 envelope taco seasoning
1 large bag taco chips
3 tomatoes, chopped
1 pound cheddar cheese or
  processed cheese, grated
1 large head lettuce, chopped

Brown ground beef and drain. Add taco seasoning. Mix well.

Just before serving, mix all ingredients in large bowl. Black olives and chopped onion may be added for additional color and flavor. This salad does not keep well.

Serves 6.

Taco Salad

1 pound hamburger
8 ounces grated
  cheddar cheese
1 can kidney beans, drained
1 or 2 tomatoes, chopped
Chopped onion to taste
1 head lettuce, torn up
1 bag (½ pound)
  Doritos, crushed
2 chopped avocadoes
  (optional)
Taco sauce to taste
Thousand Island Dressing,
  about 1 cup

Brown hamburger. Drain fat. Chill. First 5 ingredients can be combined a few hours before serving. At last minute, add lettuce, Doritos and avocadoes. Mix taco sauce into Thousand Island dressing to taste. Toss with all ingredients.

Serves 10.

Favorite Sauerkraut Salad

1 can sauerkraut, rinsed
and drained
1 can green beans, drained
1 can wax beans, drained
2 cups sliced celery
1 medium onion, chopped
1 small jar pimento
1 green pepper, chopped
1 tablespoon vegetable oil
1 cup vinegar
1½ cups sugar

Combine vegetables.
Combine oil, vinegar and
sugar. Bring to a boil. Cool.
Pour over vegetables.

Refrigerate. Can make a day
or two in advance.

Serves 10 to 12.

Scandinavian Salad

*This may also be served on hearty dark bread,
on a lettuce leaf, as an open-faced sandwich.*

1 box frozen peas
3 carrots, grated
6 ounces small shrimp,
frozen or canned
½ cup mayonnaise or
salad dressing
Salt
Pepper
Dill weed
Squeeze of lemon juice

Combine peas, carrots and
shrimp. To mayonnaise, add salt,
pepper, dill weed, and lemon
juice to taste. Combine with
peas, carrots and shrimp.

Serves 4.

Middle Eastern Lentil Salad

A wonderful vegetarian protein source with a Middle Eastern flavor.

1 cup dried lentils

4 cups water

½ cup olive oil

5 tablespoons fresh
lemon juice

3 tablespoons minced
fresh parsley

2 cloves garlic, crushed

¾ teaspoon ground cumin

1 teaspoon salt

¼ teaspoon freshly
ground pepper

Bring lentils and water to a boil. Reduce heat. Simmer, uncovered, until lentils are firm-tender (about 30 minutes).

Whisk remaining ingredients in a bowl. Drain lentils well. While still warm, add lentils to the dressing. Toss well. Arrange on a plate. May sprinkle with coriander (optional).

Refrigerate, covered, for at least 3 hours or overnight.

Tuna Salad

2 6½-ounce cans tuna, drained

3 green onions, chopped

3 stalks celery, chopped

Dressing
½ cup mayonnaise

½ cup sour cream

2 tablespoons vinegar

2 tablespoons sugar

1 teaspoon salt

1 cup chow mein noodles

Combine dressing ingredients. Toss with tuna, onions and celery. When ready to serve, add chow mein noodles. Serve on lettuce.

Serves 4.

Make-Ahead Seafood Salad

This main course salad makes a delightful lunch or supper with chips and relishes.

¾ pound white bread slices

1 7-ounce can crab meat, flaked

1 7-ounce can shrimp

2 hard-cooked eggs, chopped

1½ cups mayonnaise

½ teaspoon salt

4 teaspoons lemon juice

¼ teaspoon dill weed

Sprinkle of curry

Trim bread crusts from bread. Cut bread into ½-inch cubes. Mix with crab, shrimp and eggs. Add seasonings to mayonnaise. Mix well. Combine all ingredients. Pat into 9-by-9-inch pan.

Chill overnight. Cut into squares. Serve on lettuce. Garnish for color with paprika or snipped parsley.

Serves 6 to 8.

Freelancer's Rice Salad

Leftover rice can be used as a base for a salad of leftovers.
Your own taste, and available ingredients, will determine the outcome.

2 cups cooked rice

¼ cup salad dressing (French, Italian, etc.)

Seasoned salt, to taste

Vegetables of your choice (tomatoes, green peppers, cauliflower, zucchini, celery, broccoli, etc.)

Mix rice, dressing and seasonings. Add chopped and diced vegetables.

Shrimp Salad
This can be made the day before serving.

2 cups shell macaroni, cooked

1 green pepper, chopped

1 medium onion, diced

2 10-ounce packages
frozen small shrimp

1 small jar stuffed
olives, sliced

Dressing

3 egg yolks, well beaten

1¼ cups sugar

¾ cup vinegar

1 tablespoon flour

1 tablespoon cornstarch

Salt and pepper to taste

Cook dressing ingredients until thick. Cool. Mix with salad ingredients. Cover. Refrigerate.

Serves 8 to 10.

Coca-Cola Salad
Refreshing … different.

1 3-ounce package
orange JELL-O

1 3-ounce package cream
cheese, softened

10 ounces Coca-Cola

½ cup chopped nuts

Blend dry JELL-O into cream cheese. Heat Coca-Cola to boiling point. Pour over mixture. Mix. Add nuts. Pour into mold or bowl. Let sit for 1 to 2 hours before putting in refrigerator. Salad should separate into three layers.

Serves 4.

Cherry Delight

1 6-ounce package
  cherry JELL-O
1 8-ounce container
  Cool Whip
1 can pitted sweet cherries
  (reserve juice for liquid
  in JELL-O)

Prepare JELL-O according to package directions, substituting reserved cherry juice for some of the water. When partially set, whip JELL-O and Cool Whip together until smooth. Stir in drained cherries. Chill.

Serves 8 to 10.

Easy Fruit Salad

1 13½-ounce can chunk
  pineapple, drained
1 16-ounce can pears or
  peaches, drained and cubed
1 11-ounce can mandarin
  oranges, drained
1 22-ounce can peach or
  apricot pie filling

Mix all ingredients. Refrigerate several hours before serving.

This recipe is very flexible. It can be used successfully with miniature marshmallows, sliced bananas, grapes, melon pieces, and many other fresh fruits . . . experiment!

Serves 6 to 8.

Mandarin-Orange Salad

2 11-ounce cans
  mandarin oranges

2 cups liquid

1 6-ounce package
  orange gelatin

1 pint orange sherbet

Drain juice from oranges. Add water to juice to make 2 cups liquid. Bring liquid to a boil. Pour over gelatin. Stir until dissolved. Add sherbet.

Allow mixture to partially set. Stir in oranges. Pour into 9-by-9-inch glass pan. Chill until firm. Cut into squares. Serve on lettuce.

Serves 9.

Mandarin-Cashew Salad
Delicious!

2 heads lettuce, broken into
  bite-sized pieces

3 11-ounce cans mandarin
  oranges, drained

1 cup salted cashew nuts

1 medium onion, thinly sliced
  and divided into rings

Oil and vinegar salad dressing

Combine lettuce, oranges, nuts and onion rings. Toss with oil and vinegar dressing, just before serving.

Serves 10 to 12.

Blueberry Salad

Easy, rather sweet, purple, and very good.

2 3-ounce packages
strawberry JELL-O

2 cups boiling water

1 can blueberry pie filling

1 cup sour cream, at room
temperature

Dissolve JELL-O in boiling water. Cool. Add blueberry filling and sour cream. Mix thoroughly. Chill.

Serves 8 to 10.

Fruity Strawberry Salad

A refreshing salad, dense with fruit,
that does not easily melt on a plate with warm foods.

6 ounces strawberry-flavored
gelatin

2 cups boiling water

10-ounce package frozen
strawberries, partially
thawed

1 20-ounce can crushed
pineapple, drained

2 cups mashed bananas
(3 large bananas)

Dissolve gelatin in boiling water. Add strawberries. Stir until strawberries thaw. Add drained pineapple and bananas. Chill.

Serves 10 to 12.

Quick Molded Salad

1 3-ounce package
  lemon JELL-O
1 cup boiling water
1 10-ounce package
  frozen raspberries
1 10-ounce can mandarin
  oranges, drained

Dissolve JELL-O in boiling water. Add raspberries. Add mandarin oranges. Mix well. Pour into 1-quart mold. Chill. Salad is ready to serve in about 2 hours.

Serves 6 to 8.

Simple Low-Calorie Salad

1 box (2 envelopes) D-Zerta
  lime gelatin dessert
1½ cups boiling water
½ cup cold water
1 20-ounce can crushed
  pineapple, unsweetened
1 20-ounce can pineapple
  chunks, unsweetened
½–1 cup nuts

Dissolve gelatin (both envelopes) in boiling water. Add cold water. Stir in crushed and chunky pineapple. Add nuts. Pour into 9-by-9-inch glass pan.

Chill until firm. Cut into squares. Serve on lettuce. Garnish with non-dairy whipped topping, if desired.

Serves 9.

Frozen Fruit Salad

1 16-ounce container
sour cream

½ cup sugar

2 tablespoons lemon juice

1 8-ounce jar maraschino
cherries, drained and halved

1 16-ounce can chunky fruit
cocktail, light

1 20-ounce can crushed
pineapple, unsweetened

1 cup chopped nuts

3–4 bananas

Mix all ingredients. Place paper baking cups in muffin tins. Fill ¾ full.

Freeze until solid. Remove and store in freezer bag. Use as needed.

Makes 36 servings.

French Dressing
A favorite!

1 cup vegetable oil

1 cup sugar

½ cup vinegar

1 small onion, diced

1½ teaspoons salt

½ cup ketchup

½ cup chili sauce

Combine all ingredients. Mix well.

Store in jar in refrigerator.

Strawberry-Sour Cream Dressing

Delicious mixed with fruit as a salad, or as a topping on fresh fruit dessert.

2 cups sour cream

1 teaspoon salt

½ cup frozen strawberries, thawed

Combine sour cream and salt. Fold strawberries into sour cream mixture.

Cole Slaw with Cooked Dressing

This should be made several hours before eating,
so it is ideal to make in the morning for the evening meal.

1 small head cabbage, shredded

1 small onion, diced

2 carrots, shredded

1 tablespoon celery seed

Salt to taste

Dressing

¾ cup vinegar

1¼ cups sugar

¾ cup vegetable oil

Combine cabbage, onion, carrots, celery seed and salt.

Combine dressing ingredients in saucepan. Bring to a boil. Pour over cabbage mixture.

Refrigerate at least 3 hours.

Frozen Cole Slaw

This will also keep well in the refrigerator for a week, if you choose not to freeze it.

1 medium head cabbage, shredded

1 teaspoon salt

2 stalks celery, chopped

1 green pepper, chopped

2 carrots, grated

Dressing

1 cup vinegar

½ cup water

1½ cups sugar

1 teaspoon celery seed

1 teaspoon mustard seed

Mix salt with shredded cabbage. Let stand 1 hour. Drain any liquid. Add celery, pepper and carrots.

Combine vinegar, water, sugar, celery seed and mustard seed. Boil for 1 minute. Cool and pour over cabbage. Freeze. Remove from freezer about 2 hours before serving.

Serves 6 to 8.

Overnite Cole Slaw

A cole slaw with good staying power.

1 head cabbage, grated

2 carrots, grated

1 small green pepper, diced

1 small jar pimento, cut up

1 small onion, finely grated

Dressing

1 cup sugar

1 cup vinegar

½ teaspoon salt

½ teaspoon celery seed

Mix first 5 ingredients.

Combine dressing ingredients. Bring to a boil. While hot, pour over vegetables. Let stand overnight.

Cabbage Slaw

1 head cabbage, shredded
1 green pepper, chopped
1 2-ounce jar pimento, cut up

Dressing
1¼ cups sugar
¾ cup vinegar
1 teaspoon celery seed
1 teaspoon mustard seed
½ teaspoon salt

Mix salad ingredients.
Combine dressing ingredients.
Toss with salad.

Refrigerate overnight.

Serves 10 to 12.

Cabin German Potato Salad

1 chopped onion
5–6 bacon strips, cut
   into pieces
2 16-ounce cans German
   potato salad
2 tablespoons brown sugar

Brown onion and bacon pieces.
Add potato salad.

Heat thoroughly. Sprinkle
brown sugar on top. Heat
5 minutes longer.

Serves 5 to 6.

Old-Fashioned Potato Salad

Very good—and this recipe eliminates the guessing when seasoning.
Make it early in the day, and have this part of the dinner finished!

2½–3 cups cooked potatoes, peeled and cubed

1 teaspoon vinegar

1 teaspoon sugar

½ cup sliced celery

2 hard-cooked eggs, chopped

⅓ cup finely chopped onion

1 teaspoon salt

¾ teaspoon celery seed

¾ cup mayonnaise

Parsley and 1 hard-cooked egg, sliced, for garnish

Sprinkle potatoes, while warm, with vinegar and sugar. Toss with a fork. Set aside for 1 hour or so.

Add celery and chopped eggs to potatoes. Mix onion and seasonings into mayonnaise. Toss to mix. Refrigerate to thoroughly chill.

Serves 6.

Main Dishes

Calico Bean Casserole

This is a favorite meal of many cabin chefs.

½ pound bacon, diced

2 pounds ground beef

1 cup chopped onions

1 cup chopped celery

1 16-ounce can baked beans
in tomato sauce

1 15½-ounce can
kidney beans

1 16-ounce can
lima beans, drained

1 15½-ounce can
butter beans, drained

1 cup ketchup

3 tablespoons vinegar

1 teaspoon dry mustard

½ cup brown sugar

1 teaspoon salt

Fry bacon pieces and remove from grease. Brown beef. Add onions and celery at end of browning. In a baking dish combine remaining ingredients, including bacon. Add beef mixture.

Bake, covered, at 350° for 45 minutes. You may also cook in a crock pot on low heat for 6 to 8 hours. Keeps refrigerated for days, and freezes well.

Serves 10 to 12.

Corn Sausage Casserole

1 pound bulk pork sausage

4 eggs, beaten

2½ cups cream style corn

1 cup bread crumbs

1 teaspoon salt

⅛ teaspoon pepper

¼–½ cup ketchup

Brown sausage. Drain. Mix all ingredients, except ketchup. Pour into greased 10-by-6-inch casserole.

Bake, uncovered, at 350° for 30 minutes. Spread ketchup on top. Bake for 10 minutes more.

Serves 6.

Dried Beef Casserole

Allow at least 4 hours for this recipe.

1 10½-ounce can cream of mushroom soup

1 cup milk

1 cup grated cheddar cheese

3 tablespoons finely chopped onion

1 cup elbow macaroni, cooked

¼ pound dried beef, soaked in boiling water and drained

2 hard-cooked eggs, diced

Stir soup to creamy consistency. Stir in remaining ingredients, except eggs. Gently fold in eggs. Put in buttered 2-quart casserole. Refrigerate at least 3 hours, or overnight.

Bake, uncovered, for 1 hour at 350°.

Serves 4 to 6.

Easy Chili

1 pound hamburger, seasoned

1 onion, chopped

1 cup chopped celery

2 cans kidney beans or chili beans, drained

1 48-ounce can tomato juice

1 teaspoon chili powder (optional)

Brown onion with hamburger. Drain grease. Combine all ingredients in large kettle. Simmer for at least 1 hour.

Serves 4 to 6.

Chicken-Vegetable-French Fry Casserole

This provides meat, potatoes and vegetables in one dish. Put together ahead of time, and it's ready to eat 35 minutes after popping in the oven.

2 fryer chickens, cut up

¼ cup (½ stick) butter

¼ cup flour

1 teaspoon salt

2 cups reserved chicken broth

1 10½-ounce can cream of celery soup

1 10-ounce package frozen peas and carrots

½ cup (1 stick) butter

1 pound box frozen French fries

Parmesan cheese

Cook, cool and debone chicken. Save 2 cups of broth. (This much could be done before going to the cabin.) In a buttered 9-by-13-inch pan, or lasagna pan, put good-sized pieces of chicken.

Melt butter; add flour, salt, broth and soup. Cook until thick and smooth. Cook peas and carrots for 3 minutes. Drain. Mix with sauce and pour over chicken.

Melt stick of butter, and stir frozen French fries in it until coated. Place on top of other ingredients. Sprinkle generously with Parmesan.

Bake, uncovered, at 450° for 20 to 25 minutes. If it has been put together earlier and refrigerated, bake for 35 minutes.

Serves 8.

Hamburger-Wild Rice Casserole

This can be refrigerated or frozen before it is baked.

1 cup wild rice, washed

4 cups boiling water

¼ cup chopped onion

1½ pounds ground beef

1 10½-ounce can cream of mushroom soup

1 10½-ounce can cream of chicken soup

1 can mushrooms, drained

1 can water chestnuts, drained and sliced

2 beef bouillon cubes in 1 cup boiling water

Put rice in kettle and cover with boiling water. Simmer for 5 minutes. Remove from heat, and let stand 15 minutes before draining. Brown onion and ground beef. Drain grease. Combine all ingredients. Season to taste with salt, onion salt, paprika, celery salt, etc.

Bake at 350° for 1½ hours, covering for first half of baking, then uncovering. This "holds well" in oven—it can bake for up to 3 hours.

Serves 12.

Easy Stove-Top Stew For 4

1 pound stew meat

1 teaspoon salt

1 10½-ounce can tomato soup

1 can water

3 carrots, chopped

3 potatoes, chopped

3 small onions, chopped

Brown meat in small amount of cooking oil in a large frying pan. Add salt. Stir in soup and water.

Cover and simmer 1½ hours. Add carrots, potatoes and onions. Cook for 30 minutes more. If there is not enough juice, add water.

Serves 4.

Can Opener Casserole

1 10½-ounce can cream of
mushroom soup

1 10½-ounce can cream of
chicken soup

1 small can evaporated milk

2 6½-ounce cans
boned chicken

1 4½-ounce can
mushrooms, drained

1 cup chopped celery
(sautéed in butter)

2 cups Chinese noodles

Slivered almonds

1 small jar pimento

Combine first 7 ingredients,
and place in 1½-quart
casserole.

Bake, covered, at 350° for
1 hour. Before serving,
garnish with slivered
almonds and red pimento.

Serves 6 to 8.

Cabin Stew
No need to brown the meat.

2 pounds stew meat, cubed

1 20-ounce can tomatoes

1 box frozen peas

6 carrots, sliced

3 small onions, chopped, or
1 small jar onions and juice

1 cup celery, chopped

3 medium potatoes, diced

2 tablespoons sugar

1 tablespoon salt

¼ teaspoon pepper

¼ cup quick tapioca

1 5-ounce can water chestnuts, drained and sliced

¼ cup dry red wine

Put all ingredients in casserole.
Stir to blend. Cover.

Bake at 275° for 5 hours or
longer. Freezes well.

Serves 8.

Hunters' Stew
A traditional fall meal at the lake.

4 slices bacon, cut into
1-inch pieces

1 tablespoon butter or
margarine

1 pound lean beef for stewing,
cut into 1-inch cubes

2 large onions (2 cups),
chopped

3 medium-sized apples
(2 cups), pared, quartered,
cored and chopped

1 10½-ounce can beef broth

2 cups water

1½ teaspoons salt

2 cups carrots, pared
and diced

1 pound Polish sausage, cut
into 1½-inch lengths

1 small head cabbage
(4 cups), shredded

Cook bacon in a heavy kettle or Dutch oven until crisp. Remove with a slotted spoon, and set aside. Drain on paper towels. Add butter to drippings in kettle. Add beef, in batches, turning to brown well on all sides. Stir in onion and apple. Cook about 5 minutes or until apple is tender. Add beef broth, water and salt. Cover.

Simmer 1 hour and 20 minutes. Add carrots and sausage. Simmer 30 minutes longer. Add cabbage and reserved bacon. Simmer 10 minutes, or until cabbage is tender.

May be cooked in a crock pot for 6 hours on high, or 8 hours on low. All ingredients may be placed in the crock pot at the same time.

Variation: Omit the cabbage, and use 1½ pounds beef and ½ pound Polish sausage.

Old Tyme Beef Stew

This freezes well. You might want to double the recipe.

2 pounds beef chuck, cut into bite-sized pieces

2 tablespoons oil

4 cups boiling water

1 tablespoon lemon juice

1 teaspoon Worcestershire sauce

1 clove garlic, on toothpick

1 medium onion, sliced

1–2 bay leaves

1 tablespoon salt

1 teaspoon sugar

½ teaspoon pepper

4 large carrots, sliced

4 large potatoes, diced

Brown meat in oil. Add all ingredients except carrots and potatoes. Cover. Simmer for 2 hours, stirring occasionally. Remove bay leaves and garlic. Add carrots and potatoes.

Cover and cook 30 minutes, or until vegetables are done. Remove meat and vegetables. Skim excess fat. Thicken liquid for gravy by mixing ½ cup water and ¼ cup flour and adding slowly to meat stock. Cook for 5 minutes, until thickened, and pour over vegetables—or vegetables can be returned to gravy and mixed together.

Make at home, and take to the cabin for reheating.

Chow Mein

May be made ahead and reheated.

2 pounds chow mein meat
(pork and veal)

1½ cups (or more)
chopped celery

1 large onion, chopped

1 can bean sprouts, drained
(juice reserved)

1 can sliced water chestnuts

Fresh mushrooms, sliced

1 beef bouillon cube, in
½ cup boiling water

1 10½-ounce can cream of
mushroom soup

1 can mushroom steak sauce

1 tablespoon molasses

3 tablespoons soy sauce

2 tablespoons cornstarch

Brown meat, seasoning with
quite a bit of pepper, but no
salt. Add remaining ingredients, except cornstarch.

Simmer, covered, 1 to
1¼ hours. Thicken with
cornstarch and small portion
of bean sprout juice. Serve over
rice or chow mein noodles.

Serves 6 to 8.

Chow Mein Hot Dish

1 pound ground beef

2 cups diced celery

3 medium-sized onions,
chopped

1 cup raw rice

2½ cups hot water

1 10½-ounce can cream of
mushroom soup

4 tablespoons soy sauce

1 tablespoon brown sugar

½ pound salted peanuts

Sauté beef, celery and onions.
Drain grease. Add remaining
ingredients, except peanuts.

Bake, uncovered, at 400° for
1 hour. After 45 minutes of
baking, cover top with salted
peanuts. Continue baking for
another 15 minutes.

Serves 8 to 10.

Chopstix Tuna

1 10½-ounce can cream of
mushroom soup

¼ cup water

2 cups chow mein noodles,
divided

1 6½-ounce can white tuna,
water packed, drained

1 cup sliced celery

¼ cup chopped onion

½ cup salted cashews

Dash of pepper

Combine soup and water. Add
1 cup noodles, tuna, celery,
onion, cashews and pepper.
Place in 1½-quart casserole.
Sprinkle 1 cup noodles over
the top.

Bake, uncovered, at 375° for
15 minutes. May garnish with
mandarin orange slices.

Serves 4.

Ground Beef Stir-Fry

Excellent for "drop-ins" or when you don't know what time your eaters will arrive.

2 tablespoons oil

1½ pounds ground beef

¼ cup soy sauce

1 green pepper, cut up

3 carrots, thinly sliced

2 onions, sliced and cut
into half rings

4 stalks celery, sliced
diagonally

Fresh or canned mushrooms

1 tablespoon cornstarch

½ cup beef consommé
(freeze the rest for later use)

Stir-fry ground beef in hot
oil in fry pan or wok (450° in
electric fry pan). When meat
is brown, add soy sauce and
vegetables. Cover, and cook
5 to 8 minutes, until tender-
crisp, stirring occasionally.

Dissolve cornstarch in consommé. Add to meat and
vegetables to thicken.
Season with salt and pepper.
Serve over cooked rice.

Serves 6.

Cheeseburger Pie

1 pound ground beef
1½ cups chopped onion
½ teaspoon salt
¼ teaspoon pepper
1 cup (4 ounces) shredded
  cheddar cheese
1½ cups milk
¾ cup Bisquick
3 eggs

Lightly grease a 10-inch pie plate. Cook and stir ground beef and onion until beef is brown. Drain. Stir in salt and pepper. Spread in pie plate. Sprinkle with cheese.

Beat remaining ingredients until smooth, 15 seconds in blender on high speed or 1 minute with hand beater. Pour into pie plate.

Bake at 400° about 30 minutes, until golden brown. Let stand 5 minutes before cutting. Refrigerate any remaining pie.

Note: If using a 9-inch pie plate, decrease milk to 1 cup, Bisquick to ½ cup and eggs to 2.

Serves 6 to 8.

Good and Easy Spaghetti Sauce

1 package spaghetti sauce mix
1 pound hamburger, browned
Black olives, sliced
Celery, sliced
Fresh mushrooms, sliced
Green pepper, chopped

Follow directions on the package of spaghetti sauce mix. Add the rest of the ingredients to it. Serve over cooked spaghetti.

Spaghetti Pie

A do-ahead main dish.

6 ounces spaghetti

2 tablespoons butter

½ cup grated Parmesan cheese

2 eggs, well beaten

1 pound hamburger

½ cup finely chopped green onion

¼ cup chopped green pepper

½ cup cut-up tomatoes (fresh or canned)

1 6-ounce can tomato paste

1 teaspoon sugar

1 teaspoon oregano

½ teaspoon garlic salt

1 cup cottage cheese

½ cup shredded mozzarella cheese

Stir butter into spaghetti, which has been cooked, drained and rinsed. Add Parmesan and eggs. Form this into a crust in a buttered 10-inch pie pan.

Cook beef, onion and green pepper. Drain. Stir in tomatoes, tomato paste, sugar, oregano and garlic salt. Spread cottage cheese over spaghetti crust. Cover with meat and tomato mixture. Top with mozzarella cheese. At this point, pie can be frozen or refrigerated.

Bake, uncovered, at 350° for 30 minutes (longer, if frozen), or until bubbly. Recipe can easily be doubled.

Serves 6.

Make-Ahead Spaghetti Sauce/Chili Base

Freeze in meal-sized containers.

4 pounds ground beef

2 cups chopped onions

1 cup chopped green pepper

2 cups chopped celery

16 ounces tomato sauce

12 ounces tomato paste

4 cups tomatoes
(fresh or canned)

2 tablespoons sugar

2 teaspoons salt

2 cloves garlic (on toothpicks, for removal)

2 bay leaves

½ teaspoon oregano

Brown the beef. Midway through the browning, add onions, pepper and celery. When meat is browned, drain the grease. Add remaining ingredients. Simmer for 2 hours. Remove garlic and bay leaves.

Freeze this spaghetti sauce, if you wish. To transform this into chili, add chili powder and cans of chili beans or kidney beans (drained) to taste.

Meat Balls

1 bouillon cube

½ cup hot water

½ cup milk

1 cup soft bread crumbs

2 pounds ground beef

½ cup chopped onion, or
2 tablespoons instant onion

1 teaspoon sugar

1 teaspoon seasoned salt

1 egg

1 10½–ounce can cream of mushroom soup

Combine bouillon cube and hot water. Add other ingredients, except soup Make small meatballs. Place on cookie sheet.

Bake in 350° oven for 30 minutes. Place meatballs in baking dish, and spread with slightly diluted soup. Bake 30 minutes more. Freezes well.

Serves 6 to 8.

One-Pan Spaghetti

Time-saver spaghetti! One pan and no precooking of noodles.
Celery loaf or Italian bread goes well with this dish.

1 pound ground beef

½ cup chopped onion, or
   2 tablespoons onion flakes

1 9-ounce can whole
   tomatoes

1 18-ounce can tomato juice

1 8-ounce can tomato sauce

1½ teaspoons sugar

1½ teaspoons oregano

¾ teaspoon garlic powder

1 teaspoon
   Worcestershire sauce

½ teaspoon salt

Half of a 7-ounce package
   spaghetti, uncooked and
   broken

Brown beef and onion in a large saucepan. Drain fat. Add the tomatoes, tomato juice, tomato sauce, and the seasonings. Bring the mixture to a boil. Add the uncooked spaghetti, and lower heat to simmer.

Cover tightly, and simmer for 40 minutes, stirring occasionally. Uncover, and simmer for 15 minutes. Or bake, covered, at 325° for 1 hour, stirring occasionally. Uncover, and bake ½ hour longer. Parmesan cheese can be sprinkled on top just before serving.

Serves 4 to 6.

Meat and Macaroni Dinner

1 pound ground beef

¼ cup chopped onion

1 cup elbow macaroni,
   cooked and drained

1 10½-ounce can cheddar
   cheese soup

⅓ cup water

¼ teaspoon pepper

Cook meat and onion in large skillet until onion is tender. Drain fat. Add remaining ingredients. Heat thoroughly, and serve.

Serves 4.

Do-Ahead Lasagna

This recipe can be made ahead of time and left in the refrigerator all day.
The uncooked noodles make it super for saving—time and pans!

1 pound ground beef

1 tablespoon instant chopped onion

2 teaspoons salt

1 tablespoon sugar

1 teaspoon chili powder

1 teaspoon garlic salt

1½ teaspoons basil or oregano

1 12-ounce can tomato paste

1 15-ounce can tomato sauce

3½ cups water

¾ pound (2¼ cups) shredded cheese (American or mozzarella)

¾ pound lasagna noodles, uncooked

Brown ground beef with onion and seasonings. Add tomato paste, tomato sauce and water. Bring to a boil, simmer 10 minutes. (Mixture will be thin.)

In 9-by-13-inch baking pan, ladle about 1½ cups sauce. Cover sauce with 4 uncooked noodles. Ladle more sauce to cover noodles. Sprinkle ⅓ of cheese over sauce. Make 3 layers like this. Cover with foil.

Bake at 350° for 1½ hours, or for 2 hours if it has been refrigerated.

Park Rapids Goo

Fast and easy.

1 pound ground beef

1 small onion, chopped (optional)

1 14¾-ounce can Franco-American spaghetti

Parmesan cheese

Fry hamburger with onion. Drain grease. Add spaghetti. Heat thoroughly. Sprinkle with Parmesan cheese.

Serves 4.

Pot Roast Meat Loaf

1 pound lean ground beef

⅔ cup evaporated milk

⅓ cup fine bread crumbs

¼ cup ketchup

1 teaspoon salt

2 teaspoons Worcestershire sauce

Dash of pepper

2 teaspoons dried parsley flakes

3 medium potatoes, peeled and sliced

3 medium onions, sliced

3 medium carrots, sliced

1 teaspoon salt

Combine all ingredients, except parsley flakes, vegetables and salt. Shape into loaf. Place in 9-by-13-inch pan. Place vegetables in layers around meat. Sprinkle with parsley flakes and salt. Cover with foil.

Bake at 375° for 1 hour, or until vegetables are tender. Remove foil. Bake 10 minutes longer.

Serves 4.

Good Neighbor's Hot Dish with Sour Cream

1 cup chopped onion

2 tablespoons margarine

1½ pounds ground beef

3 cups medium noodles, uncooked

3 cups tomato juice

1 teaspoon salt

1½ teaspoons celery salt

Dash of pepper

2 teaspoons Worcestershire sauce

¼ green pepper, chopped

1 3-ounce can sliced mushrooms (optional)

1 cup sour cream

Brown onion and ground beef in margarine. Add remaining ingredients, except sour cream.

Cook in large, heavy fry pan on medium heat until noodles are tender. Add sour cream. Heat through.

Serves 8.

Knobby Pines Goulash

When our family of 14 gets together at the lake for a reunion,
a double recipe of goulash is one of our favorite Saturday night meals.

1½ pounds ground beef

1½ cups chopped celery

2 onions, chopped

2 beef bouillon cubes

½ cup hot water

1 10½-ounce can tomato soup

1 16-ounce can stewed
tomatoes

1 7-ounce package cooked
egg noodles

Garlic salt, to taste

Onion salt, to taste

1 8-ounce can water
chestnuts, drained and
sliced (optional)

Brown meat, celery and onions.
Drain. Dissolve bouillon cubes
in water. Add soup, tomatoes,
noodles and seasoning. Pour
into 2-quart casserole.

Cover, and bake at 350° for
1 hour. Add water chestnuts
the last ½ hour of baking time.

Serves 8 generously.

Swedish Meatballs

Freezes well.

1 pound ground beef

½ cup fine bread crumbs

1 egg

⅔ cup milk

¼ cup finely chopped onion

½ teaspoon salt

⅛ teaspoon pepper

¼ teaspoon nutmeg

1 10½-ounce can cream of mushroom soup

Combine all ingredients, except soup. Form into small balls.

Brown slowly. Pour off fat. Place in 1-quart casserole. Dilute soup with ¼ cup water. Pour mixture over meatballs.

Bake at 325° for 1 hour, or 375° for ½ hour.

Taco Pie

This recipe may be doubled. Put in a 9-by-13-inch pan, and it will serve at least 10 people.

1 can refrigerated crescent rolls

1 small or medium package taco chips, crushed

1 pound ground beef

1 8-ounce can tomato sauce

½ can (½ cup) water

1 package taco seasoning

1 cup sour cream

1 cup mozzarella cheese, shredded

Brown the beef. Drain fat. Add tomato sauce, water and taco seasoning. Place crescent rolls in bottom of 10-inch pie plate. Layer other ingredients on top, in this order: ½ of crushed taco chips; ground beef mixture; sour cream; mozzarella cheese; remaining taco chips.

Bake at 375° for 25 minutes.

Serves 6.

Aunt Linnea's Five-Decker Dinner

This entire meal is made in an electric fry pan!

6 slices of bacon, cut into 1-inch pieces

1 pound ground beef, made into 4 patties

Salt and pepper to taste

4 onions, sliced

4 medium potatoes, sliced

4–6 carrots, sliced

¼ cup chopped green pepper

1 tablespoon chopped parsley (optional)

¼ cup water

Separate bacon squares, and place on bottom of fry pan. Put ground beef patties on the bacon. Salt and pepper. Layer the onions, potatoes and carrots over this, seasoning with salt and pepper. Put green pepper and parsley on top.

Cook on medium heat until bacon is sizzling, 3 to 5 minutes. Add water. Cover. Turn heat to low. Cook about 45 minutes. Drain grease. Recipe can be increased; cook a little longer.

Serves 4.

Texas Straw Hats

Shredded cheese, sour cream and black olives can be served separately, allowing guests to add what they wish to the meat mixture.

1 cup chopped onion

⅔ cup chopped celery

⅔ cup chopped green pepper

3 tablespoons oil

2 pounds ground beef

2–3 teaspoons chili powder

2 teaspoons salt

¼ teaspoon pepper

2 6-ounce cans tomato paste

½ cup ketchup

2 cups water

2 teaspoons Worcestershire sauce

Dash Tabasco sauce

2 6-ounce packages corn chips

Shredded sharp American cheese

In large skillet, cook onions, celery and green pepper in oil until tender. Brown beef separately. Drain fat. Mix beef with onion, celery and green pepper. Add remaining ingredients, except chips and cheese.

Simmer, uncovered, for 1 hour, stirring occasionally. Serve on corn chips. Top generously with cheese. Keeps refrigerated for several days.

Serves 6.

Salmon Loaf

1-pound can red salmon

¼ cup shortening

1 teaspoon chopped onion

1½ cups soft bread cubes

½ teaspoon salt

¼ teaspoon black pepper

1 egg, slightly beaten

Salmon juice plus milk to
  make 1 cup

1 teaspoon lemon juice

¼ teaspoon lemon rind

1 tablespoon fresh chopped
  parsley, or flakes

Flake salmon, removing large bones. Drain liquid, and add enough milk to make 1 cup. Melt shortening, and add onion. Cook until yellow. Add bread cubes and seasonings; brown. Add remaining ingredients.

Bake, uncovered, at 350° in glass loaf pan for about 45 minutes. Makes one loaf.

Serves 8.

Beans and Wieners Supreme

This dish is good served immediately, or can be reheated.
Keeps in refrigerator several days.

¼ pound bacon, diced

6 wieners, cut into 1-inch
  pieces

¼ cup chopped onion

½ cup chopped green pepper

¾ cup crushed or chunk
  pineapple, drained

1 31-ounce can pork and
  beans, drained

½ cup brown sugar, packed

1 cup ketchup

2 tablespoons
  Worcestershire sauce

Fry bacon until crisp. Add wieners, onion, pepper and pineapple. Cook and stir until onion is tender. Add remaining ingredients.

Cook over low heat for 1 hour, stirring occasionally, or bake, uncovered, at 300° for 1 hour.

Serves 8.

Lake Dogs with Beans

½ cup butter

2 tablespoons
  prepared mustard

2 tablespoons
  Parmesan cheese

1 tablespoon finely chopped
  green pepper

1 tablespoon chopped onion

8 hot dog buns

8 frankfurters

1 16-ounce can pork
  and beans

Cream butter. Add mustard, cheese, green pepper and onion. Place buns on double-thick rectangles of foil. Spread mixture on both sides of split buns. Slit franks lengthwise, but do not cut through. Place franks on buns, and fill cavity with beans. Fold foil over sandwich.

Grill for 10 minutes on each side, or bake at 350° for 15 minutes.

Serves 8.

Cabin Supper Special
Popular with children.

8 wieners

¼ cup Cheez Whiz (other
  cheese can be used)

1–2 tablespoons minced onion

2 cups mashed potatoes
  (instant is fine)

Paprika

Cook wieners, and set aside to cool somewhat. Melt cheese in top of double boiler, adding a small amount of milk to thin, if desired. Stir in minced onion. Add potatoes, and mix well. Split wieners lengthwise, and spoon potato-cheese mixture on top. Sprinkle with paprika.

Broil until lightly browned. Serves 4.

Hash Brown Brunch or Supper

⅓ cup chopped green pepper

8 slices bacon

1 box dehydrated hash browns with onions

1 teaspoon salt

1¾ cups water

1 cup grated cheddar cheese

4 large eggs

¼ cup milk

½ teaspoon salt

Dash of pepper

Parboil pepper, and reserve water for the required water. Fry bacon in large electric skillet. Remove bacon, leaving 3 to 4 tablespoons bacon grease in skillet. Set temperature to 300°. Mix potatoes, salt, water and green pepper, and pour into skillet.

Cook, uncovered, until liquid is absorbed and bottom is golden brown, about 10 minutes. Turn. Reduce temperature to 250°. Sprinkle cheese over mixture. Mix eggs, milk, salt and pepper. Pour over cheese, and cover. Cook until eggs are done and potatoes are golden brown, about 12 minutes. Garnish with bacon.

Serves 6 generously.

Ham Au Gratin

¼ cup vegetable oil

1 pound frozen hash browns

1 pound ham, cut into bite-sized pieces

1 cup plain yogurt, at room temperature

1 10½-ounce can cheddar cheese soup

½ teaspoon mustard

Heat oil and brown hash browns (cover and cook 4 minutes; uncover and cook 8 minutes, or until golden). Put hash browns in buttered 9-inch-square baking pan. Cover with ham cubes. Combine yogurt, soup and mustard. Pour over casserole.

Bake at 400° for 20 to 25 minutes.

Serves 4 to 6.

Chicken/Broccoli, Minnesota Style

1 chicken, cut up, or chicken breasts (3½ pounds)

3 10-ounce packages frozen broccoli

1 10½-ounce can cream of mushroom soup

2 10½-ounce cans cream of chicken soup

1 4½-ounce can mushrooms, drained

Parmesan cheese

In a kettle, cook chicken with a small amount of water, until tender. Remove skin and bones. Cut chicken into small pieces. Cook broccoli until not quite done.

Alternate layers of chicken and broccoli in a 9-by-13-inch pan. In a bowl, mix the 3 cans of soup with 1½ soup cans of water. Add drained mushrooms. Pour over chicken and broccoli. Sprinkle with Parmesan cheese.

Bake for 1 hour at 325°.

Serves 10 to 12.

Zucchini Crescent Pie

MMMMMMMMMMM-good!

4 cups thinly sliced,
   unpeeled zucchini

1 cup coarsely chopped onion

½ cup margarine or butter

½ cup chopped parsley or
   2 tablespoons parsley flakes

½ teaspoon salt

¼ teaspoon black pepper

¼ teaspoon garlic powder
   (or salt)

¼ teaspoon sweet basil leaves

¼ teaspoon oregano leaves

2 eggs, well beaten

8 ounces (2 cups) shredded
   mozzarella cheese

1 8-ounce can refrigerated
   crescent dinner rolls

2 teaspoons Dijon
   prepared mustard

In a 10-inch skillet, cook zucchini and onion in margarine until tender—about 10 minutes. In a large bowl, combine parsley and seasonings. Blend in eggs and cheese. Stir in vegetable mixture.

Separate dough into 8 triangles. Place in ungreased 11-inch quiche pan or 10-inch pie pan. Press over bottom and up sides to form crust. Spread mustard onto crust. Pour vegetable mixture evenly into crust.

Bake at 375° (350° for glass dish) for 18 to 20 minutes.

Serves 6.

Chicken and Stuffing Hot Dish

A special treat for cabin guests.

1 6-ounce box chicken-flavored Stove Top stuffing mix

1 10-ounce package frozen broccoli spears

3 chicken breasts

1 10½-ounce can cream of chicken soup

1 cup grated Colby cheese

Prepare stuffing mix according to directions on the box. Slightly cook the broccoli spears. Cook the chicken breasts and cut into bite-sized pieces. Mix the soup with 1 soup can water. Layer all ingredients, in order listed, in a 7½-by-11½-inch greased baking dish. Cover with foil.

Bake at 350° for 30 minutes.

Serves 8.

Meat, Fish & Poultry

Hamburger Stroganoff

Serve over rice, buttered noodles or boiled potatoes.
If there are any leftovers, serve on toast for a quick lunch.

2 pounds hamburger, seasoned

2 medium onions

1 large can mushrooms, drained (reserve juice)

1 10½-ounce can cream of mushroom soup

1 10½-ounce can tomato soup

1 pint sour cream

Brown hamburger. Drain fat. Sauté onions in mushroom juice; drain. Mix all ingredients. Simmer. Can reheat over low heat when needed.

Serves 8 to 10.

Make-Ahead Hamburgers

Do your own thing! Recipe is not explicit, but the burgers will be good.

Hamburger patties

Barbecue sauce

Using your favorite hamburger or meatloaf recipe, shape mixture into hamburger patties.

Fry. (At this point, the hamburgers may be refrigerated or frozen.) Place hamburgers in a baking dish or roaster. Pour barbecue sauce over them. Cover.

Heat in oven. Serve on buns.

Pot Roast Supreme

Tender and delicious. Works well with less expensive cuts of beef.

1 beef roast (about 3 pounds)

Flour

6 carrots, peeled

6 potatoes, peeled

1 10½-ounce can onion soup, heated

Dredge meat with flour on both sides. Brown the roast. No seasoning necessary. Add carrots and potatoes to roast. Pour heated soup over all.

Bake, covered, at 275° for 4 hours.

Serves 6.

Beef Brisket

This is tasty and tender.

3–4 pounds beef brisket, rinsed and patted dry

3 tablespoons brown (apple cider) vinegar

Accent

Lawry's seasoned salt

Lots of paprika

Garlic salt

1 onion, sliced

Sprinkle all ingredients on top of meat.

Bake, uncovered, at 350° for 1 hour. Add 2 cups hot water. Cover.

Bake 3 to 4 hours longer. Slice thin and serve.

Serves 10 to 12.

Barbecued Beef Brisket

This can be started a few days before serving.

6 pounds beef brisket
Garlic, onion and celery salt
3 tablespoons liquid smoke
Salt and pepper
Worcestershire sauce
18-ounce bottle
  barbecue sauce

Sprinkle all sides of brisket with flavored salts. Place brisket in glass dish. Pour liquid smoke on meat. Cover and refrigerate overnight. Before baking, sprinkle meat with flavored salts, salt, pepper and Worcestershire sauce.

Bake, covered, at 250° for 5 hours. (May be done ahead to this point and refrigerated for later reheating.) Slice thin. Add barbecue sauce. Bake at 250° for 1½ hours. May thicken sauce with flour.

Serves 12 to 15.

Salisbury Steak

2 pounds ground beef
½ cup bread crumbs
⅔ cup beef bouillon
2 teaspoons instant
  chopped onions
1 egg
2 teaspoons salt

Mix all ingredients well. Portion and shape into 8 steaks.

Bake at 350° for 10 to 15 minutes.

Grilled Flank Steak

*Put meat in marinade at home, and take to destination
in a plastic bag in your cooler. Good with baked potatoes and cole slaw.*

1½–2 pounds flank steak
¼ cup soy sauce
3 tablespoons honey
½ teaspoon ginger
½ cup salad oil
2 tablespoons vinegar
½ teaspoon garlic powder

Lightly score flank steak against the grain. Marinate in the rest of the ingredients for 24 to 48 hours. Keep in a covered glass pan or in a plastic bag in a bowl or pan in the refrigerator.

Grill for 5 to 7 minutes per side. Slice thin, across the grain

Serves about 3 people per pound of meat.

Pork Tenderloin Stacks

4 slices pork tenderloin or pork chops
4 slices sweet onion
4 slices tomato
4 slices American cheese
2 slices bacon, cut in half

Brown the tenderloin slices, seasoning to taste. Stack on remaining ingredients, in order listed, skewering together with a toothpick. Place in pan or casserole. Cover.

Bake at 350° for 1½ hours. Uncover after 1 hour, so bacon will become crisp.

Serves 4.

Cheese-Stuffed Patties

1 pound ground beef
½ teaspoon salt
Dash pepper
American cheese, shredded
Chopped onion
Bottled barbecue sauce

Mix ground beef, salt and pepper. Divide meat into 6 portions and pat them out ¼-inch-thick between sheets of waxed paper. Place small amount of cheese, onion and barbecue sauce in centers of 3 patties. Top with remaining meat patties. Press around edges to seal.

Grill over medium-hot coals for about 7 minutes on each side, or broil.

Makes 3 burgers.

Liver and Vegetables, Pennsylvania Dutch Style

Aunt Gladys recommends this for all liver lovers.

1 pound beef liver, cut into
  serving pieces
Flour
1 small onion, sliced
4 potatoes, quartered
4 carrots, split lengthwise
Salt and pepper to taste
1 cup water

Dip liver into flour. Brown both sides in heavy frying pan or electric skillet (with tight-fitting lid). Add onions, potatoes, carrots, and salt and pepper. Pour water over ingredients. Cover tightly.

Simmer for 1 hour, or until carrots and potatoes are done.

Serves 4 to 5.

Florida Pork Chops

4 pork chops or 2 pork steaks (do not pre-brown)

1 cup orange juice

¼ cup brown sugar

1 teaspoon salt

1 teaspoon dry mustard

¼ teaspoon pepper (lemon pepper or fresh-ground is best)

Place pork chops in an 8-inch-square baking dish. Mix remaining ingredients. Pour over top of chops. Add additional orange juice, if needed, to cover.

Bake at 350° for 1¼ hours.

Serves 2 or 4.

Hinds Lake Fish with Sesame Butter

2 pounds northern pike or walleye

Salt and pepper

½ cup butter, melted, divided

4 tablespoons lemon juice

Dash Worcestershire sauce

6 tablespoons toasted sesame seeds

Lemon quarters

Parsley

Arrange fish in well-buttered shallow baking dish. Season with salt and pepper. Brush with some of the melted butter.

Bake at 350° for 20 minutes, or until fish flakes easily when tested with a fork.

Heat remaining butter until very lightly brown. Add lemon juice and Worcestershire sauce. Stir in sesame seeds. Spoon over baked fish. Serve with lemon quarters and parsley.

Joe's Crappies
This one is hard to beat.

Crappies
Soda crackers
Flour
Margarine
Vegetable oil

Salt both sides of fillets and let them rest awhile. Crush soda crackers and put into a plastic bag. Add some flour to bag of crumbs, if desired. Heat frying pan with half margarine and half vegetable oil. Drop fillets into plastic bag, and shake well.

Fry fillets quickly until tender. Place on paper towels to drain. If fillets cannot be cooked within 24 hours, freeze in plastic containers of water.

Fish Fillets Almondine
Serve your catch for dinner tonight.

Fish fillets, fresh or frozen, thawed (walleye, northern pike or bass)
2 tablespoons butter or margarine per fillet
1 teaspoon lemon juice per fillet
Paprika
Lemon pepper
Bread crumbs, very fine
Almonds, slivers or slices

Arrange fillets in 9-by-9-inch baking dish. Melt butter. Add lemon juice. Pour over fillets. Cover the fillets completely. Sprinkle with paprika, lemon pepper and bread crumbs.

Bake at 450° for 8 to 15 minutes, or until fish flakes easily Add almonds the last 2 minutes. Watch carefully.

Serves 4.

Northern Pike, Swedish Style

Clean the fish by slitting the underside, scaling and removing the innards. Place fish in a large pan, and cover halfway with water. Add peppercorns, a bay leaf and a sliced onion. Bring to a boil.

Boil gently for 10 minutes. With spatulas, carefully turn fish over, and cook for another 10 minutes. Remove fish and arrange in a curved shape on a plate. Peel back the skin. Serve with one or more of the following garnishes: melted butter, horseradish or grated hard-cooked eggs.

Honey-Fried Walleye Fillets

6 large walleye fillets
⅔ cup vegetable oil
1 egg, lightly beaten
1 teaspoon honey
1½ cups coarsely crushed soda crackers
½ cup flour
½ teaspoon salt
½ teaspoon pepper

Dry fillets on paper towel. Heat oil in a 10-inch skillet. Combine and mix the egg and honey. Dip fillets into the mixture. Then, coat with a mixture of cracker crumbs, flour, salt and pepper, pressing crumbs firmly into fillets.

Fry about 3 minutes on each side in preheated oil.

Serves 6.

Easy Baked Fish

Celery soup provides a new taste in this fish recipe.

⅓ cup butter or margarine

12–14 cleaned panfish, fresh or frozen

1 10½-ounce can cream of celery soup

½ cup lemon juice

¼ cup parsley flakes, dehydrated

Melt butter in 9-by-13-inch pan. Arrange fish in butter. Pour other ingredients, in order listed, over fish.

Bake at 350° for 50 minutes, or until fish flakes easily.

Serves 6.

Caesar's Fillets

Attention all microwave owners—try this recipe with your next catch.

1 pound fish fillets

½ cup Caesar salad dressing

½ cup seasoned bread crumbs

½ cup shredded cheddar cheese

Dry fish fillets well. Moisten thoroughly with Caesar dressing. Lay single layer in a microwave pan. Cover with bread crumbs. Top with cheddar cheese. Cover.

Microwave on high until fish flakes easily with a fork, or until cheese is melted. Check after 5 minutes. Let stand a minute. Check again.

Serves 2 to 3.

Sweet and Sour Chicken Wings

These tasty chicken wings may be used as an appetizer or for a light meal. Delicious served hot or cold. Bake at home and take to your destination in the cooler—will keep for several days.

20 to 25 chicken wings

1 cup soy sauce

1 cup pineapple juice

1 teaspoon garlic powder

1 cup water

1 cup sugar

¼ cup salad oil

1 teaspoon ground ginger

Cut each wing in half. Discard tips. Combine all ingredients. Pour over wings in shallow baking pan. Refrigerate at least 1 hour, but overnight is better. Remove wings from sauce and place on baking sheet.

Bake, uncovered, at 350° for 1 to 1¼ hours, or until brown and tender.

Glazed Chicken

Easy and tasty!

1 fryer chicken, cut up, or 4 chicken breasts with skin on

8-ounce bottle Russian dressing

1 cup apricot preserves (or orange marmalade)

1 package dry onion soup

Combine dressing, preserves and dry soup. Pour over chicken in baking dish.

Bake, uncovered, at 350° for 1 to 1½ hours, or until fork-tender. Baste occasionally while baking.

Tarragon Chicken

This is good, hot or cold.

2 broiler-fryer chickens, cut into serving pieces

½ cup melted butter or margarine

Salt

Pepper

Paprika

Chili powder

Dried tarragon

Melt butter or margarine in shallow baking pan. Place chicken, skin side down, in pan. Sprinkle with salt, pepper, paprika, chili powder and 1 teaspoon tarragon.

Place under broiler, about 5 inches from heat. Broil for about 15 minutes. Turn pieces over, repeat sprinkling of seasonings. Broil again for 15 minutes. Remove from broiler, and cover pan tightly with foil.

Bake at 325° for 25 to 30 minutes.

Serves 5 to 6.

Honey Chicken

Good with rice, peas, and a green salad containing mandarin orange slices.

3 pounds chicken, cut up
4 tablespoons butter
½ cup honey
¼ cup prepared mustard
1 teaspoon salt
1 teaspoon curry powder

Wash and dry chicken. Remove skin, if desired. Melt butter and mix in remaining ingredients. Roll chicken in mixture to coat. Arrange meaty side up in a single layer. Cover with remaining sauce.

Bake at 375° for 1 hour, or until chicken is tender and glazed.

Chinese Chicken

Delish!

⅓ cup soy sauce
2 tablespoons oil
1 teaspoon dry mustard
½ teaspoon ginger
¼ teaspoon pepper
1 clove garlic, minced
1 fryer, cut up

Combine first 6 ingredients. Brush over washed and drained chicken parts. Let stand ½ hour, and again brush with sauce. Put in shallow pan, or on rack if crisp chicken is desired.

Bake in 375° oven for about 50 minutes. Brush with sauce every 15 minutes.

Drippings may be used as gravy on potatoes or biscuits. Sauce may be made ahead of time and stored in a jar.

Parmesan Chicken

Delicious hot or cold. Easy to make ahead of time.

2 chickens, skinned and
  cut up
1 cup butter, melted
2 cups Italian bread crumbs
1 cup grated Parmesan cheese
¼ teaspoon instant
  minced garlic
½ teaspoon, or more, salt
2 tablespoons parsley flakes

Melt butter in pan. Combine bread crumbs, Parmesan cheese, garlic, salt and parsley flakes. Dip chicken pieces into butter. Roll in crumb mixture. Arrange in pan.

Bake, uncovered, at 375° for 1 hour.

Serves 6 to 8.

Delicious Easy Chicken

Chicken can be assembled, covered and refrigerated the night before baking. Bake as directed.

6 to 8 chicken breasts, split
  and deboned
1 10½-ounce can cream of
  mushroom soup
½ cup sour cream
¼ cup Hellmann's
  mayonnaise
¼ cup dry white vermouth

Combine soup, sour cream, mayonnaise and vermouth. Pour over chicken breasts, which have been rolled and placed seam side down in greased casserole or 9-by-13-inch pan.

Bake, uncovered, at 250° for 2½ to 3 hours. Wild or white rice would be a good accompaniment.

Serves 6 to 8.

Breast of Chicken on Rice

1 10½-ounce can cream of mushroom soup

1 soup can milk

¾ cup uncooked white rice (½ of this can be wild rice)

1 4-ounce can mushroom stems and pieces, plus liquid

1 envelope onion soup mix

3 chicken breasts, boneless, cut in half (or a 2½-pound chicken, cut up)

Mix the mushroom soup with milk. Reserve ½ cup of this mixture for later use. Combine soup mixture with the rice, mushrooms and liquid and ½ of the onion soup mix. Pour into an oblong baking dish or 7½-by-11½-inch pan. Place breasts on top. Pour the reserved soup mixture over the chicken breasts. Sprinkle with the rest of the onion soup mix. Cover.

Bake at 350° for 1 hour. Uncover, and bake 15 minutes longer.

Serves 6.

Crock Pot Goose or Duck

Our family jokes: If the goose is not tender after 6 or 7 hours of cooking, add 1 quart of red wine. Cook 1 hour longer. Discard the goose and drink the juice!

1 duck or goose, cut up

1 teaspoon Morton's seasoning salt

Lawry's seasoning salt

Accent

2 oranges, quartered

2 apples, quartered

2 stalks celery, chopped

2 carrots, chopped

1 onion, chopped

Put 3 cups water in crock pot. Add Morton's seasoning. Sprinkle Lawry's and/or Accent on meat pieces. Put meat into crock pot.

Cook on high for at least 2 hours (longer if game is frozen). Turn to low. Continue cooking for 4 to 5 hours, or until done. Discard vegetables. Serve with orange sauce. (See page 203.)

Vegetables & Side Dishes

Dilly Beans

This relish will keep in the refrigerator for several weeks.

Fresh green beans
½ cup white vinegar
½ cup water
¼–½ cup sugar
1 teaspoon dry dill weed, or
   3 heads fresh dill

Wash the beans and cut off ends. Cut into pieces, if desired. Boil in unsalted water for 3 to 5 minutes, until just tender. Blanch in ice water.

Mix vinegar, water, sugar and dill weed. Pour over beans. Store in covered container in the refrigerator.

German Green Beans

1 can (about 1 pound) green
   beans, mostly drained
2 slices bacon, cut up
1 green onion, cut up
   (or onion salt)
1 tablespoon vinegar
Parmesan cheese

Fry bacon. Add beans to bacon and grease. Add onion and vinegar. Heat thoroughly. Put in serving bowl, sprinkle with Parmesan cheese.

Serves 3 to 4.

Bestemor's Baked Beans for a Crowd

Delicious! Recipe may easily be cut in half.

6 16-ounce cans Bush's
  baked beans

1½ pounds ground beef

1 pound bacon, cut into
  small pieces

3 4-ounce cans
  mushrooms, drained

1½ cups ketchup

1 cup brown sugar

2 teaspoons dry mustard

Brown the ground beef. Fry
bacon. Drain fat. Combine
all ingredients.

Bake at 325° until thoroughly
heated—about 1 hour. Can
also be heated in a crock pot,
for 4 hours or longer.

Serves 18 to 20.

Easy Baked Beans

2 1-pound cans baked beans
  in tomato sauce

1 teaspoon dry mustard

¾ cup brown sugar

½ cup ketchup

6 slices bacon, cut up

Mix mustard and brown sugar.
Layer the beans and the sugar
mixture in baking dish. Pour
ketchup over the top. Sprinkle
with bacon pieces.

Bake at 325° for 3 hours.

Serves 6 to 8.

Broccoli Supreme

1 20-ounce bag frozen
chopped broccoli

1 10½-ounce can cream of
chicken soup

2 carrots, grated

½ cup (4 ounces) sour cream

½ 2.8-ounce can French fried
onions or croutons

Cook broccoli according to package instructions. Drain. Mix with soup, carrots, sour cream and fried onions. Turn into lightly greased medium-sized casserole.

Bake at 350° for 30 minutes.

Serves 6 to 8.

Baked Corn

1 16-ounce can cream
style corn

1 16-ounce can whole
kernel corn, drained

1 egg, beaten

½ cup bread or
cracker crumbs

½ cup sour cream

½ teaspoon salt

Dash of pepper

Combine all ingredients. Mix well. Put in buttered casserole.

Bake at 350° for about 40 minutes, or until firm.

Serves 6.

Hot Fruit Compote

A colorful addition to any meal. Excellent!

1 16-ounce can apricots, quartered

1 16-ounce can sliced peaches

1 15¼-ounce can pineapple chunks

1 14-ounce jar apple rings, quartered

1 16-ounce can pear halves, quartered

½ cup butter

½ cup sugar

2 tablespoons flour

1 cup golden sherry

Drain fruit, and arrange in large casserole or 9-by-13-inch baking dish. Heat butter, sugar and flour until thick as cream. Add sherry. Pour over fruit, and let stand in refrigerator at least 8 hours or up to 24 hours.

Bake, covered, at 350° for 25 minutes and uncovered for 5 to 10 minutes. Serve immediately. Keeps up to one week in refrigerator.

Cucumber Sidecar

Excellent with fish.

2 or 3 cucumbers, peeled and sliced

1 small onion, chopped

2 heaping tablespoons mayonnaise or salad dressing

2 tablespoons sugar

½ teaspoon celery seed

Salt and pepper to taste

Combine cucumbers and onion. Add remaining ingredients. Stir into vegetables. Can make about 1 hour before mealtime.

Scandinavian Cucumbers

½ cup sour cream

1 tablespoon sugar

2 tablespoons snipped parsley

2 tablespoons tarragon vinegar

1 tablespoon finely chopped onion

¼ teaspoon dried dill weed

2 or 3 small cucumbers, thinly sliced

Mix all ingredients, except cucumbers. Fold mixture into cucumbers.

Cover, and chill for 2 hours.

Cucumber Relish

8 cucumbers, peeled and sliced as thin as possible

1 onion, sliced very thin

1 cup vinegar

1½ cups sugar

2 tablespoons salt

Combine vinegar, sugar and salt. Pour over cucumbers and onions. Refrigerate overnight before serving. Keeps well up to 20 days, when refrigerated.

Carrots and Celery, Simply Together

Colorful, tasty and low-cal!
You decide how much to serve, and prepare accordingly.

Sliced carrots

Sliced celery

Instant chicken bouillon granules

Bring water—enough so that it covers vegetables—to a boil. Add about 1 teaspoon bouillon granules for each cup of water. Add vegetables. Simmer just until tender.

Cauliflower and Carrots

1 small head cauliflower, broken into small pieces

2–3 carrots, sliced

1 10½-ounce can cream of chicken soup, undiluted

2 cups grated cheddar cheese

1 cup bread crumbs

Cook cauliflower and carrots until just tender. In a greased 2-quart casserole, layer half of vegetables, soup and cheese. Repeat layering. Cover top with bread crumbs.

Bake at 350° for 30 minutes, or until bubbly.

Cream of celery or cream of mushroom soup may be used as a substitute.

Serves 6.

Carrot-Cheese-Rice Casserole

2 cups cooked rice

2½ cups grated carrots

⅓ pound grated Colby or cheddar cheese

2 eggs, beaten

¼ cup milk

1 tablespoon butter, softened

¼ cup chopped onion

1 teaspoon salt

⅛ teaspoon pepper

Mix all ingredients. Pour into a 1½-quart casserole.

Bake at 350° for 45 minutes to 1 hour, or until carrots are done.

Serves 6.

Carrots with Apples and Honey
A surprisingly tasty combination.

1 pound (2 cups) carrots
1 teaspoon salt
1 teaspoon lemon juice
⅔ cup honey
1¾ cups diced apples

Peel carrots, split into halves, and slice about ¼-inch thick. Place carrots in saucepan and cover with water.

Boil gently until tender. Drain liquid, reserving 2 tablespoons. Add salt, lemon juice and honey to the 2 tablespoons of reserved liquid. Add diced apples.

Simmer gently for about 10 minutes. Add carrots. Simmer until apples are tender, about 5 minutes.

Serves 4 to 6.

Savory Grilled Onions
May be prepared in advance and cooked at your picnic site.

1 medium-to-large onion
**   per person**
Granulated beef bouillon

Peel and core onion. Set onion on 12-inch square of aluminum foil. Fill center of onion with bouillon. Seal edges of foil.

Place on charcoal grill for 30 to 45 minutes, turning occasionally.

Granny's Grits
Margaret and Jack's favorite from the ol' South.

1 cup quick-cooking grits

4 cups water

1½ teaspoons salt

½ cup margarine

1 cup Longhorn
cheese, grated, divided

4 eggs

1 cup milk

Pepper

Cook grits, water and salt according to directions on the grits package. Add margarine and ¾ cup cheese to grits. Let cook slightly. Add lightly beaten eggs, milk and pepper. Stir until well mixed. Pour into 1½-quart casserole. Top with remaining cheese.

Bake at 350° for 1 hour.

Serves 6.

Fried Green Tomatoes
Can't wait until your tomatoes ripen? Try these.

4 medium green tomatoes,
cut into thick slices

½ cup flour

4 tablespoons bacon grease,
or oil

Dredge each side of tomato slices with flour. Fry in hot grease, turning to brown both sides. Sprinkle with salt and pepper.

Dilled Peas
Dill-icious!

¼ cup water
2 beef bouillon cubes
3 tablespoons butter
1 teaspoon finely
  chopped onion
¼ teaspoon dill weed
Pepper
2 10-ounce packages
  frozen peas

Bring water to a boil. Blend in beef cubes, butter, onion, dill and pepper. Add peas. Return to boil.

Simmer until tender, about 5 minutes.

Serves 6.

Peas To Please

⅓ cup butter or margarine
3 or 4 whole green onions
1 box frozen peas

Melt butter in heavy saucepan. Place green onions, tops and all, in saucepan. Add frozen peas. Do not add water.

Cook slowly until peas are crispy-tender, about 15 to 20 minutes. Season with salt and pepper. Discard onions, and serve.

Zucchini Casserole
You'll be asked for this recipe!

3 pounds zucchini

3 onions, chopped

1 stick butter

½ pound fresh mushrooms (canned mushrooms are OK)

Sauce

2 tablespoons butter, melted

½ cup grated cheddar cheese

1 teaspoon seasoned salt

1 cup sour cream

Topping

2 tablespoons grated cheddar cheese

Crushed Ritz crackers

Slice zucchini into thin slices. Parboil in salted water, uncovered. Drain. Sauté onions in butter. Add mushrooms, and sauté.

Add cheese, seasoned salt and sour cream to melted butter. Mix with vegetables, and heat through. Pour into 1½- or 2-quart casserole.

Sprinkle topping over all.

Bake, uncovered, at 350° for 30 minutes.

Serves 8.

Rice Casserole
A good side dish that freezes well.

1 cup raw rice

1 10-ounce package chopped broccoli

4 tablespoons margarine

1 small onion, chopped

½ cup chopped celery

1 10½-ounce can cream of chicken soup

1 8-ounce jar Cheez Whiz

Cook rice with no salt. Cook broccoli until tender and drain. Fry onion and celery in margarine until tender. Combine rice, broccoli, soup, Cheez Whiz, onion and celery.

Bake at 350° for 30 minutes.

Serves 6.

Easy Rice Casserole

*This is a delicious accompaniment to beef. A double recipe fits
nicely into a crock pot. Rice can be reheated in a crock pot for serving.*

1½ cups converted rice,
uncooked

1 10½-ounce can beef
consommé

1 10½-ounce can onion soup

8 ounces canned mushrooms
and juice

¼ pound butter

⅓ cup Parmesan cheese

Combine and mix
all ingredients.

Bake, uncovered, at 350°
for 1 hour. Stir occasionally.
For a double recipe, bake
about 1 hour and 25 minutes,
or until rice is absorbed.
Can also prepare by cooking
in a covered crock pot for
5 to 6 hours.

Noodles and Rice Casserole

½ cup margarine

½ pound fine egg noodles

2 cups uncooked minute rice

2 10½-ounce cans
Campbell's onion broth
or soup

2 10½-ounce cans
chicken broth

4 tablespoons soy sauce

1 8-ounce can water
chestnuts, sliced

1 4-ounce can mushroom
pieces (optional)

Melt margarine in large skillet.
Add uncooked noodles.
Cook until brown, stirring
constantly. Add uncooked rice
and remaining ingredients. Mix
well. Put in 3-quart casserole.

Bake, uncovered, at 350°
for 45 minutes, stirring
occasionally.

Serves 10 to 12.

Wild Rice Casserole

1 cup wild rice, raw

½ onion, chopped

2 tablespoons butter or margarine

3 chicken bouillon cubes

¼ cup hot water

1 10½-ounce can cream of mushroom soup

1 soup can water

2 3½-ounce cans mushrooms, drained, or fresh mushrooms

Wash and drain the rice. Sauté onion in butter or margarine. Dissolve chicken bouillon cubes in ¼ cup hot water. Combine all ingredients in casserole.

Bake at 325° for 1½ to 2 hours. Do not overcook. This may accompany a main meat dish, or ¼ to 1 pound of ground beef (browned) may be added. Freezes well.

Serves 6 to 8.

Rice and Fresh Mushrooms

½ cup butter, melted

1½ cups raw rice

1 10½-ounce can beef consommé

1 10½-ounce can onion soup

½ pound fresh mushrooms, sliced

8 ounces (2 cups) shredded sharp cheddar cheese

Melt butter in 1½-quart pan. Add rice, soups and mushrooms. Pour into 11-by-7-by-l-inch baking dish.

Bake at 350° for about 1 hour. Sprinkle with cheese for the last few minutes of baking.

Sweet/Sour Vegetables

Double the recipe, and carry to the lake in an ice cream pail.

½ bunch broccoli, cut into bite-sized pieces

½ head cauliflower, cut into small flowerettes

2 carrots, sliced

2 zucchini (cucumber-sized), sliced

1 large mild onion, sliced

Dressing

1½ cups cider vinegar, heated

⅓ cup sugar

¼ cup salad oil

1 teaspoon salt

Mix dressing ingredients. Pour over vegetables. Toss. Cover, and chill overnight. Good for several days in the refrigerator.

Add button mushrooms and ripe olives to dress it up for company.

Serves 6 to 8.

Sliced Baked Potatoes

Easy and popular.

Baking potatoes (1 per person)

Butter (about 4 tablespoons for a 9-by-13-inch pan)

Parmesan cheese (optional)

Peel potatoes. Slice lengthwise into ¼-inch-thick slices. Melt butter in pan in oven. Put potatoes in pan, and turn them over, coating both sides with the butter.

Bake at 400° for 30 minutes, or 350° for 40 minutes. Sprinkle with salt before serving. Can also sprinkle with Parmesan cheese.

Sunshine Lemon Potatoes

Great with fish. Different, very good and easy!

3 large potatoes, thinly sliced

¼ cup melted butter

1 tablespoon freshly squeezed lemon juice

2 teaspoons freshly grated lemon peel

3 tablespoons Parmesan cheese (can substitute seasoned croutons)

½ teaspoon paprika

Arrange potatoes in 9-by-13-inch baking dish. Combine butter and lemon juice. Brush over potatoes. Combine lemon peel, cheese and paprika. Sprinkle over potatoes.

Bake at 350° for 45 minutes. Serves 4.

Scalloped Potatoes

This recipe does not have precise amounts. It's one of those wonderful dishes that you can prepare for any number of people. Somehow, the whipping cream and water combination will not curdle or become watery.

Sliced raw potatoes

Whipping cream

Salt and pepper

Parmesan cheese (optional)

Layer potatoes in baking dish, sprinkling salt and pepper on them rather generously. Using equal parts of whipping cream and water, pour over potatoes, covering about ⅔ depth of potatoes. Sprinkle with Parmesan cheese.

Bake, uncovered, at 350° for about 1 hour, or until done.

Mashed Potato Casserole

Put together at home and bake at the lake.
Mash your potatoes in advance, without the last-minute fuss.

5 pounds red potatoes,
  peeled and cooked

1 8-ounce package cream
  cheese, softened

1 cup half-and-half

½ cup butter, melted

1 teaspoon salt

1 teaspoon onion salt

¼ teaspoon paprika

Combine cream cheese with half-and-half, beating until well blended. Add well drained potatoes. Mash, blending well. Add salt, onion salt and all but 1 tablespoon of the melted butter. Put into a 2-quart casserole. Brush with the tablespoon of butter. Sprinkle with paprika.

If baking immediately, bake at 350° for 30 minutes. If refrigerated for later baking, bake at 350° for 45 minutes.

Serves 12 to 15.

Potato Casserole

3 cups half-and-half

1 cup skim milk

½ cup butter, melted

⅔ cup Parmesan cheese

1 teaspoon salt

2 pounds Ore Ida southern
  style frozen hash browns

Combine half-and-half, milk and cooled butter in 2-quart glass casserole. Add cheese, salt and hash browns.

Bake, covered, at 325° for 45 minutes. Remove cover. Bake 15 minutes more.

Serves 6 to 8.

Vermicelli in a Fry Pan

An excellent meat accompaniment.

½ pound butter
1½ 7-ounce packages
  vermicelli
1 cup dry Minute Rice
2 10½-ounce cans onion soup
1 cup sliced mushrooms
4 green onions, chopped
  (include tops)

Melt butter in a large fry pan. Add dry (uncooked) vermicelli, and fry until brown. Add dry rice, and brown a little longer. Add soup and enough water to make a total of 3 cups of liquid.

Cover, and simmer for 20 minutes. Stir, and add mushrooms and green onions. Cover, and cook another 20 minutes Add more water if necessary.

Serves 8.

Fried Apple Rings

A tasty accompaniment to ham, sausage or pork.

Tart apples
Butter
Brown sugar or grated cheese

Core the apples. Peel only if the skins are tough. Slice into ½-inch rings.

Sauté in butter until barely tender. Turn over. When apples are nearly tender, sprinkle lightly with brown sugar or grated cheese. Cover, and cook until the sugar or cheese melts.

Desserts

Red Grape Dessert
For dessert, or snack, or brunch, or ...

1 pound seedless red grapes
¼ cup sour cream
¼ cup cream cheese, softened
2 tablespoons sugar

Combine sour cream, cream cheese and sugar. Fold into grapes. Refrigerate for a few hours before serving. Keeps well for a few days in the refrigerator. Serve in small bowls.

Serves 4 to 6.

Fresh Fruit Compote
Can be used at any meal.

Fresh fruit, a variety
Sugar
¼ cup orange liqueur or
**   kirsch (optional)**

Prepare a variety of fresh, seasonal fruit. Arrange in layers in a glass bowl, sprinkling sugar lightly over each layer. Spoon liqueur over each layer for flavor, if you choose. Toss gently, and chill for 2 or more hours.

Some suggested fruits: peaches, nectarines, blueberries, strawberries, cantaloupe, honeydew, grapes, watermelon.

Cantaloupe with Blueberry Yogurt

Pretty!

Cut cantaloupe into wedges. Top each wedge with a generous dollop of blueberry yogurt.

Frozen Grapes

A frosty treat for a hot summer day. Appreciated by dieters.

Green or red seedless grapes

Wash grapes and remove stems. Drain on paper towels. Freeze in a single layer. When frozen, transfer to plastic bag or other container. Eat and enjoy.

Orange Strawberry Dessert

1 6-ounce can frozen orange juice concentrate, thawed

¾ cup sugar

1 pint strawberries, washed, hulled and halved

6 oranges, peeled and sectioned

Mix thawed concentrate and sugar. Let stand several minutes, until sugar is dissolved. Combine strawberries and orange sections. Pour concentrate mixture over fruit. Mix well. Refrigerate several hours or overnight.

Serves 6.

Heavenly Summer Fruit Delight

**Raspberries, blueberries,
strawberries, peaches or
whatever fruit you like**

Sour cream

Brown sugar

Spoon a dollop of cold sour
cream (about 1 heaping tablespoon per serving) on top of
cold, clean fruit. Sprinkle
generously with brown sugar.

Frozen Fruit Cup

*Versatile! This can be a breakfast fruit, a lunch dessert or a dinner salad.
Great to have on hand for unexpected guests.*

**2 10-ounce packages frozen
strawberries, thawed**

**1 16-ounce can apricots,
drained and cut up**

**1 20-ounce can crushed
pineapple, not drained**

4 bananas, diced

Syrup
2 cups sugar

1 cup water

Mix fruit.

Bring sugar and water to a boil.
Cool. Pour over the mixed
fruit. Ladle into individual serving dishes. Freeze. Cover with
foil when frozen. Remove
from freezer 35 to 45 minutes
before serving. Paper soufflé
cups or 5-ounce plastic glasses
make good serving dishes.

Makes 15 to 25 individual
servings, depending upon size
of serving dish.

Blueberry-Green Grape Combo

2 cups blueberries
2 cups green grapes
¾ cup sour cream
¼ cup brown sugar

Combine sour cream and brown sugar. Toss with fruit. Put into 4 serving dishes. Sprinkle with brown sugar for garnish. Chill before serving.

Serves 4.

Orange Take-Along Cake

1¼ cups boiling water
1 cup quick-cooking oats
½ cup butter or margarine, softened
1 cup granulated sugar
½ cup brown sugar
2 eggs
½ cup frozen orange juice concentrate, thawed and undiluted
1 teaspoon vanilla
1¾ cups flour
1 teaspoon baking powder
1 teaspoon baking soda
½ teaspoon salt
½ teaspoon cinnamon
½ cup walnuts

Pour boiling water over oats. Set aside. Cream butter and sugars. Beat in eggs, one at a time. Add orange juice and vanilla. Sift dry ingredients. Blend into creamed mixture alternately with oats, beginning and ending with flour mixture. Fold in nuts. Pour into greased 9-by-13-inch pan.

Bake at 350° for 40 minutes.

Summer Fruit Favorite

½ pound (4 cups) Natural 100 cereal, or any plain granola cereal

¼ cup melted butter

2 cups sugar

¾ cup soft butter

2 eggs, beaten

Fresh strawberries, about 1 quart, cleaned and sliced

3–4 sliced bananas

1 pint whipping cream

Blend cereal in blender. Reserve some crumbs (⅓ cup) for top. Combine cereal and melted butter. Pat into 9-by-13-inch pan. Chill.

Cream sugar and soft butter. Add eggs and blend. Pour into pan. Cover with strawberries and bananas. Whip cream and sweeten; spread over fruit. Sprinkle with remaining cereal crumbs. Refrigerate.

Note: This recipe contains uncooked eggs, which can contain *salmonella* and other bacteria.

Cheesecake

1¼ cups graham cracker crumbs

¼ cup melted butter or margarine

8 ounces cream cheese, softened

½ cup sugar

1 tablespoon lemon juice

½ teaspoon vanilla

⅛ teaspoon salt

2 eggs, beaten

1 cup sour cream

2 tablespoons sugar

½ teaspoon vanilla

Combine cracker crumbs and butter. Pat into 8-inch pie pan or 8-inch-square pan. Combine cream cheese, sugar, lemon juice, vanilla, salt and eggs. Pour into crust.

Bake at 350° for 25 to 30 minutes. Mix sour cream, sugar and vanilla. Pour over hot, baked cheese cake. Bake 10 minutes longer. Cool. Refrigerate or freeze. Can be served with fruit topping.

Serves 8.

Strawberry Cheesecake

1 graham cracker crust, made according to package directions for pie pan

1 3-ounce package strawberry JELL-O

1 cup boiling water

1 10-ounce package frozen strawberries

1 8-ounce package cream cheese, softened

1 cup sugar

1 13-ounce can evaporated milk, chilled

Chilled bowl and beaters

Pat graham cracker crust into 9-by-13-inch pan. Dissolve JELL-O in 1 cup boiling water. Add frozen strawberries. Cool. Beat cream cheese and sugar until fluffy. In separate chilled bowl, whip evaporated milk. Fold all together. Pour over crust.

Chill in refrigerator for several hours. Garnish each piece with a fresh strawberry. Freezes well. Thaw in refrigerator before serving.

Individual Cherry Cheesecakes

Serve alone or with other "finger desserts."

16 ounces cream cheese, softened

¾ cup sugar

2 eggs

1 teaspoon vanilla

24 vanilla wafers

1 can cherry pie filling

Beat cheese and sugar until creamy Add eggs and vanilla; mix well. Put a vanilla wafer in bottom of each of 24 cupcake liners. Spoon cheese mixture into each.

Bake in muffin pan at 350° for 20 minutes. Remove from tins, and cool. Top with cherry pie filling. Chill overnight before serving. Freezes well.

Serves 24.

Jiffy Shortcake
An easy base for your fresh fruit shortcakes!

1 cup self-rising flour

1 cup vanilla ice cream
softened

Mix flour and ice cream. Drop by spoonful onto ungreased cookie sheet or cake pan.

Bake at 400° for about 15 minutes, or until light brown.

Makes 6 shortcakes.

Mandarin Orange Cake
Lasts up to a week, but if people are near it, the cake will not survive!

2 11-ounce cans
mandarin oranges

2 cups flour

2 eggs

2 teaspoons baking soda

2 cups sugar

2 teaspoons vanilla

1 teaspoon salt

Glaze
1½ cups brown sugar

6 tablespoons butter

6 tablespoons milk

Remove excess liquid from oranges, but do not completely drain. Combine all cake ingredients. Beat until well blended and oranges are broken up.

Bake in 9-by-13-inch greased pan at 325° for 30 to 35 minutes.

Combine all glaze ingredients in a saucepan. Boil for 3 minutes, stirring constantly. Make holes in hot cake with fork. Pour hot glaze over cake. Serve with whipped cream.

Cranberry Bundt Cake

⅓ cup poppy seeds

1 cup warm water

1 package yellow cake mix

1 small package instant vanilla pudding

½ cup vegetable oil

4 eggs

2 cups fresh cranberries, rinsed

Soak poppy seeds in water for about 10 minutes. Mix all ingredients for 2 minutes with electric mixer.

Bake at 350° for 1 hour to 1 hour and 15 minutes in well-greased tube or Bundt pan. Cool cake in pan for 10 minutes. Remove to rack to finish cooling.

Apple Cake

¼ cup margarine

1 cup sugar

1 egg

1 cup flour

1 teaspoon baking soda

½ teaspoon salt

¾ teaspoon cinnamon

2¼ cups peeled, raw apples, coarsely grated

½ cup chopped nuts

½ cup raisins

2 teaspoons vanilla

Cream margarine, sugar and egg. Sift flour, soda, salt and cinnamon. Add the dry ingredients to the creamed mixture in thirds, blending well after each addition. Add the apples, nuts, raisins and vanilla. Stir until thoroughly mixed. Spread into greased 8-by-8-inch pan.

Bake at 350° for 45 minutes, or until toothpick inserted in center comes out clean.

Sift powdered sugar over cake, when it has cooled slightly. Serve with whipped topping, if desired.

Makes 9 to 12 servings.

Chocolate Bundt Cake
Teachers' lounge favorite.

1 box fudge brownie mix

1 box coconut almond or coconut pecan frosting mix

1 cup sour cream

⅔ cup milk

2 eggs

Combine all ingredients in a bowl. Mix well. Pour into greased and floured Bundt pan.

Bake at 350° for about 70 minutes, or until inserted toothpick comes out clean. Cool. Remove from pan. Sprinkle with powdered sugar.

Lumberjack Chocolate Sheet Cake
This big cake is moist and delicious.

2 cups sugar

2 cups flour

1 teaspoon salt

1 teaspoon baking soda

1 cup butter

1 cup water

4 tablespoons cocoa

½ cup sour cream

2 eggs

Mix sugar, flour, salt and soda. Combine the butter, water and cocoa. Bring to a boil. Add to dry mixture. Add sour cream and eggs. Pour into a greased 11-by-17-inch jelly roll pan. Bake at 375° for 15 to 18 minutes.

Frosting

1 cup butter

6 tablespoons condensed milk

2 tablespoons cocoa

1 teaspoon vanilla

1 box (scant 4 cups) powdered sugar, sifted

Combine first 4 frosting ingredients. Bring to a boil. Add powdered sugar. Beat well.

Serves 20 easily.

Date-Chocolate Picnic Cake

This moist cake has a "baked-in" topping and travels very well.

1 cup chopped dates
1½ cups boiling water
1 teaspoon baking soda
½ cup shortening
½ cup sugar
½ cup brown sugar
2 eggs
1¾ cups flour
¼ teaspoon salt
¾ teaspoon soda
6 ounces chocolate chips
½ cup brown sugar
½ cup chopped nuts

Mix dates, water and soda and let cool. Cream the shortening, sugars and eggs. Combine with date mixture and stir well. Add flour, salt and soda.

Mix chocolate chips, ½ cup brown sugar and nuts, and sprinkle on cake mixture.

Bake in 9-by-13-inch greased pan at 350° for 30 to 40 minutes.

Rhubarb Cake

½ cup shortening
1½ cups sugar
1 egg, beaten
1 teaspoon vanilla
1 cup buttermilk
1 teaspoon baking soda
2 cups flour
½ teaspoon salt
3–4 cups cut-up fresh rhubarb

Glaze
2 tablespoons butter, softened
3 tablespoons milk
1 cup sifted powdered sugar

In large mixing bowl, cream shortening and sugar. Add egg. Stir in vanilla.

Pour buttermilk into a 2-cup container. Add soda. Mix. Combine dry ingredients. Add alternately to sugar mixture with buttermilk. Fold in rhubarb. Mix well.

Bake in a 9-by-13-inch greased and floured pan at 350° for 45 minutes. Combine glaze ingredients and spread on cake.

Mississippi Mud Cake

Given by a Southern belle, Terry,
married to an Iowa farm boy and living in Minnesota.

1 cup margarine

2 cups sugar

⅓ cup cocoa

1½ cups flour

4 eggs, beaten

1 cup coconut

1 cup pecans, coarsely
chopped

1 7-ounce jar
marshmallow crème

Frosting
6 tablespoons margarine

1 square (1 ounce)
unsweetened chocolate

¼ cup milk

3 cups powdered sugar

1 teaspoon vanilla

Melt margarine. Add sugar, cocoa, flour and eggs. Beat together by hand. Fold in coconut and pecans. Pour into 9-by-13-inch greased cake pan.

Bake at 350° for 40 minutes. Remove from oven, and immediately spread marshmallow crème over cake. Let cool.

Melt margarine, chocolate and milk over low heat. Add sugar and vanilla. Spread over marshmallow crème.

Big Lake Cake

Ingredients are easy to take along.

2 cans blueberry pie filling

1 box white cake mix

1/4 pound (1 stick) butter,
melted

1 3-ounce package slivered
almonds

Put blueberry pie filling on bottom of 9-by-13-inch buttered pan. Sprinkle dry cake mix on top. Drizzle melted butter over cake mix. Sprinkle almonds on top.

Bake at 350° for 50 minutes.

Carrot Cake
Tasty and moist!

2 cups sugar

2 cups flour

2 teaspoons baking soda

2 teaspoons baking powder

2 teaspoons cinnamon

1 teaspoon salt

4 eggs, beaten

1½ cups vegetable oil

3 cups shredded carrots

½ cup chopped pecans

1 teaspoon vanilla

Frosting

6 ounces cream cheese, softened

½ stick (¼ cup) butter or margarine, softened

1 box (1 pound) powdered sugar, sifted

2 teaspoons vanilla

Combine dry ingredients. Add remaining cake ingredients, mixing well.

Bake in a greased 9-by-13-inch pan at 300° for 1 hour. Check for doneness.

Combine frosting ingredients. Mix well. Spread on cake.

Cherry Crunch
Easy, good, and fast to prepare for unexpected company!

1 21-ounce can cherry pie filling

¾ cup Bisquick

¼ cup butter or margarine, softened

½ cup sugar

½ cup chopped nuts

½ teaspoon cinnamon

Pour pie filling into an ungreased 9-inch-square pan. Combine other ingredients, and sprinkle over the cherries. Bake at 350° for 25 to 30 minutes.

Serves 6 to 8.

Crazy Cherry Cake

It's mixed in the cake pan . . . no need for a mixing bowl!

¼ cup vegetable oil

1 white cake mix

2 eggs

½ cup water

1 can cherry pie filling

Cream Cheese Frosting

1 3-ounce package cream cheese, softened

1 tablespoon milk

1 teaspoon lemon juice

Dash of salt

2½ cups powdered sugar, sifted

Spread oil around 9-by-13-inch cake pan. Add cake mix, eggs and water, combining well. Add pie filling. Mix with batter just to marbleize.

Bake at 350° for about 30 minutes, or until done.

Blend all frosting ingredients, except the sugar. Gradually add sugar, beating until smooth and of spreading consistency. If too thick, stir in additional milk, 1 teaspoon at a time.

Nötkaka

A nut cake recipe from Sweden, where they use hazel nuts. Our own pecans or walnuts will do.

3 eggs

1 cup sugar

1 6-ounce package chopped nuts

½ teaspoon baking powder

Beat eggs and sugar. Add nuts and baking powder.

Bake in well-greased and sugared 8-by-8-inch pan at 350° for 40 minutes. Serve with whipped cream.

Serves 9.

Choc-Dot Pumpkin Cake or Cupcakes

2 cups sifted all-purpose flour

2 teaspoons baking powder

1 teaspoon baking soda

½ teaspoon salt

1½ teaspoons cinnamon

½ teaspoon ground cloves

¼ teaspoon allspice

¼ teaspoon ginger

2 cups sugar

4 eggs

1 16-ounce can pumpkin

1 cup vegetable oil

1 cup All Bran cereal

1 6-ounce package
   chocolate chips

1 cup chopped nuts

Lemon glaze

2 tablespoons butter

1½ cups confectioner's sugar

2 teaspoons lemon juice

2 tablespoons orange juice

Sift flour, baking powder, soda, salt, spices and sugar. Set aside. In a large bowl, beat eggs until foamy. Add pumpkin, oil and cereal. Mix well. Add sifted dry ingredients, mixing only until combined. Stir in chocolate chips and nuts. Fill miniature greased cupcake pans ⅔ full.

Bake at 350° for 20 to 25 minutes. Cool.

Cream all glaze ingredients. Glaze cupcakes. You may also bake this recipe in a tube pan for about 70 minutes. Cool completely before removing from pan. Freezes well.

Makes about 100 small cupcakes.

Minnesota Sundae
The sweet and salty topping is a good combination!

Top vanilla ice cream with honey and sunflower seeds.

Berry Pie

This pie is especially good with wild blueberries.
Note that this crust does not require a rolling pin!

Crust
2 cups flour
1¼ teaspoons salt
2 teaspoons sugar
⅔ cup salad oil
3 tablespoons milk

Filling
4 cups berries
1 cup sugar
¼ cup flour
¼ teaspoon cinnamon
⅛ teaspoon nutmeg
⅛ teaspoon cloves
2 tablespoons margarine
or butter

Mix flour, salt, sugar, oil and milk together in 8-by-8-inch pan. Reserve 1 cup of the mixture to sprinkle on top. Pat rest in bottom of pan.

Mix berries and dry ingredients. Put over crust. Dot with margarine. Sprinkle reserved crust mixture on top. Bake at 400° for 40 to 50 minutes.

Easy Refrigerator Pie

This recipe makes two pies. No baking necessary!

2 prepared graham cracker crusts
1 6-ounce can frozen lemonade, thawed
1 14-ounce can sweetened condensed milk
1 8-ounce container Cool Whip
1 14-ounce can crushed pineapple, drained
Yellow food coloring, a few drops (optional)

Combine lemonade and milk. Add other ingredients, and mix well. Divide mixture between two pie shells. Chill at least two hours before eating. May be frozen. Delicious as is, or may top with a blueberry sauce.

These two pies will serve 12.

Chocolate Amaretto Pie

Our neighbors serve this for special guests at their cabin on Lower Cullen Lake.

1½ cups chocolate Oreo cookie crumbs

¼ cup butter, softened

1 tablespoon sugar

1 quart chocolate ice cream

⅓ cup amaretto liqueur

1 cup heavy cream

2 tablespoons amaretto chocolate sprinkles

Mix crumbs, butter and sugar. Press mixture into ungreased 9-inch pie pan. Chill. Soften ice cream. Stir in ⅓ cup amaretto. Pour into chilled pie shell. Mix cream and 2 tablespoons Amaretto. Beat until stiff. Pile whipped cream in mounds around edge of pie. Freeze. Take out 10 minutes before serving.

Serves 6 to 8.

Apple Crisp

Apples, peeled and sliced

Cinnamon

1 teaspoon salt

¼ cup water

1 cup flour

1¼ cups sugar

½ cup butter

In a 9-by-13-inch buttered pan, put enough apples to fill ¾ full. Sprinkle with cinnamon to taste, salt and water. Combine the flour, sugar and butter. Sprinkle over the apples.

Bake at 350° for 40 minutes. Serve warm with cream or ice cream.

Serves 6.

No Crust Pumpkin Pie

Serve warm with ice cream. Try butter brickle!

4 eggs
¾ cup sugar
1 teaspoon ginger
1 teaspoon cinnamon
½ teaspoon salt
1 16-ounce can pumpkin
1 cup milk

Beat eggs. Add sugar and spices. Mix in salt and pumpkin. Blend in milk and stir until mixture is smooth. Pour into greased 9-inch pie pan.

Bake at 325° for 50 minutes, until firm or when knife inserted in filling 2 inches from center comes out clean.

Apple Pie Pudding

This tastes good whether warm or cold.

2 large tart cooking apples, peeled and thinly sliced
¾ cup brown sugar
½ cup self-rising flour
¼ cup butter
½ cup chopped pecans

Arrange apples in layers in loaf pan or baking dish. Sprinkle each layer with brown sugar, using about ½ cup. Mix together remaining sugar and flour. Cream in the butter. Add pecans. Put this on top of apples.

Bake at 350° for 45 minutes. You may wish to serve this with poured cream.

Serves 4.

Brown Rice Pudding

White rice may be used instead of brown.

2 cups cooked brown rice
(a scant ¾ cup, uncooked)

3 cups milk

3 eggs, beaten

¾ cup brown sugar or honey

1 cup raisins

Sprinklings of nutmeg and/or
cinnamon (optional)

Mix all ingredients. Spread in a buttered casserole or 9-by-13-inch pan.

Bake at 350° for 1 hour. Serve in sauce dishes—pass the cream to pour over it. Good warm or cold!

Serves 10 to 12.

Frozen Chocolate Cream Pie

1 4-ounce package Baker's
German sweet chocolate

⅓ cup milk, divided

2 tablespoons sugar

1 3-ounce package cream
cheese, softened

3½ cups (1 8-ounce container)
Cool Whip, thawed

8-inch graham cracker crust

Heat chocolate and 2 table-spoons of the milk in saucepan over low heat, stirring until chocolate is melted. Beat sugar into cream cheese. Add remaining milk and the chocolate mixture. Beat until smooth. Fold in Cool Whip, blending until smooth. Spoon into crust.

Freeze until firm, about 4 hours. Garnish with chocolate curls, if desired. Remove from freezer 10 minutes before serving. Store any leftover pie in the freezer.

Favorite Refrigerator Dessert

A good choice when feeding a crowd.

1 cup flour

½ cup nuts

½ cup margarine

1 8-ounce package
  cream cheese

1 cup powdered sugar

1 large container Cool Whip

2 packages instant pudding,
  any flavor

3 cups milk

Nuts, chopped (optional)

Mix together flour and nuts. Cut in margarine, as for pie crust. Press into ungreased 9-by-13-inch pan. Bake at 350° for 15 minutes. Cool.

Cream together cream cheese and powdered sugar. Add 1 cup Cool Whip to creamed mixture. Spread over cooled crust.

Beat together instant pudding and milk. Spread over cream cheese layer. Spread remaining Cool Whip over pudding layer. Sprinkle with nuts. Refrigerate for several hours or overnight.

Serves 20.

Crème de Coffee Dessert
Simple ... and the men love it!

Coffee-flavored ice cream

Crème de cacao (liqueur
  or flavoring)

Pecans or almonds,
  well toasted

Toast nuts in advance by baking in a shallow pan at 350° for 10 to 20 minutes. For each serving of ice cream, top with 2 tablespoons of crème de cacao. Sprinkle with nuts.

Quick Summer Trifle

1 white Jiffy cake mix
  (8½ ounces)

Fresh fruit—peaches, strawberries, blueberries, etc.

1 package French vanilla
  instant pudding

3-ounce package cream
  cheese, softened

8-ounce carton Cool Whip,
  or 1 cup whipping cream,
  whipped and sweetened

Prepare cake mix according to directions. Bake at 350° in a 9-by-13-inch pan. Test for doneness after 15 minutes. When cooled, cover cake with a layer of sliced fresh fruit.

Prepare pudding according to directions, and mix with cream cheese. Spread over fruit. Cover with Cool Whip. Refrigerate.

Serves 12 to 15.

Schaum Torte
This will melt in your mouth.

Meringue Crust
4 egg whites (reserve yolks for filling)
¼ teaspoon cream of tartar
1 cup sugar

Filling
4 egg yolks, well beaten
½ cup sugar
3 tablespoons lemon juice
Lemon rind, grated, from one lemon
1 cup whipping cream
1 tablespoon powdered sugar

Beat egg whites until frothy. Add cream of tartar and beat. Gradually add sugar, beating until stiff and glossy. Spread in a well-greased pie pan. Bake for 1 hour: 275° for first 20 minutes; 300° for next 40 minutes.

Cook egg yolks, sugar, lemon juice and rind, stirring constantly, until thick. When crust and filling are cool, whip the cream, sweetening it with powdered sugar. Spread ½ of the whipped cream on the crust, then the lemon filling, and top with remaining whipped cream. Refrigerate. Can make 12 to 24 hours in advance.

Serves 6, or 8 if necessary.

Cookies & Bars

Tried-and-True Sugar Cookies

1 cup margarine, softened

1 cup powdered sugar

1 cup sugar

1 cup (scant) vegetable oil

2 eggs, well beaten

1 teaspoon vanilla

4 cups all-purpose flour

½ teaspoon salt

1 teaspoon baking soda

1 teaspoon cream of tartar

Cream margarine and sugars. Add oil, eggs and vanilla. Mix. Mix dry ingredients and stir into sugar mixture. Chill at least two hours.

Place 1-inch balls on ungreased cookie sheet. Flatten with glass dipped in sugar.

Bake at 350° for 12 to 15 minutes.

Makes about 100 cookies.

Oatmeal-Coconut Cookies

½ cup butter or margarine

½ cup shortening

1 cup sugar

1 cup brown sugar

2 eggs, beaten

1 teaspoon vanilla

1 cup flour

1½ teaspoons baking powder

1 teaspoon baking soda

½ teaspoon salt

2 cups dry oatmeal

2 cups coconut (can substitute chocolate chips or raisins)

Cream butter, shortening and sugars. Add eggs and vanilla. Sift flour, baking powder, soda and salt. Add to first mixture. Add oatmeal and coconut. Form dough into balls.

Bake at 350° until brown, about 12 minutes.

Peanut Butter Cookies

Excellent for anyone allergic to wheat—and for peanut butter lovers!

1 cup peanut butter
1 cup sugar
1 teaspoon baking powder
1 egg, beaten

Mix ingredients well. Roll into balls the size of walnuts.

Bake at 325° for about 10 minutes.

Makes about 3 dozen cookies.

Grandma's Ginger Cookies

¼ cup butter
½ cup Crisco
1 cup sugar
1 egg
1 teaspoon cinnamon
1 teaspoon cloves
1 teaspoon ginger
4 tablespoons molasses
2 teaspoons baking soda
2¼ cups flour

Cream shortenings and sugar. Add remaining ingredients. Mix together. Chill dough. Roll into size of large marble. Dip into sugar.

Bake at 350° for 10 minutes. If you want cracks on the top, sprinkle a few drops of water on each cookie before baking.

Unbaked Cookies

2 cups carob chips or
chocolate chips

1 cup peanut butter

1 6-ounce bag chow
mein noodles

Spanish peanuts or
sunflower seeds

Melt chips. Stir in peanut butter until well blended. Add chow mein noodles and nuts or seeds. Drop by tea-spoonful onto waxed paper. Let set to harden.

Moravian Sugar Cookies
A great sheet cookie. Cut after baking.

½ cup butter, softened

1 cup sugar

1 teaspoon baking powder

1 teaspoon vanilla

¼ teaspoon salt

1 egg

1¼ cups flour

Topping
¼ cup sugar

2 teaspoons cinnamon

¼ cup finely chopped nuts
(optional)

Combine butter, sugar, baking powder, vanilla and salt. Blend in egg and flour. Spread out half of dough on a well-greased cookie sheet. It will make a rectangle about 8-by-10 inches.

Combine topping ingredients and spread half of it over the dough.

Bake at 350° for 12 to 15 minutes, or until golden brown on edges. Cool 1 minute. Cut into squares or rectangles, and remove from pan while warm.

Repeat the process with remaining half of dough and topping.

Toasted Coconut Cookies
Delightfully delicious and easy to make.

2 3⅜-ounce packages instant toasted coconut pudding

1½ cups margarine

2½ cups flour

Mix all ingredients Shape into balls and flatten.

Bake at 350° for 15 minutes.

Makes 6 dozen cookies.

Soda Cracker Cookies
Very good!

35 soda crackers

1 cup brown sugar

1 cup butter

12 ounces chocolate chips

½ cup chopped walnuts

Line a 10-by-15-inch pan with foil. Place crackers on the foil. Boil the brown sugar and butter for 3 minutes. Spread over the crackers.

Bake at 400° for 5 minutes. In the meantime, melt chocolate chips. When crackers have been removed from oven and the bubbling has stopped (about 1 minute), spread melted chocolate on top. Sprinkle with nuts. Pan may be put in freezer for faster cooling. Cut or break into serving-sized pieces.

Makes about 35 pieces.

Monster Cookies

Right out of Paul Bunyan's kitchen. Get out your biggest mixing bowl!

4 cups sugar

2 cups (1 pound) margarine

2 pounds (4½ cups)
  brown sugar

3 pounds crunchy
  peanut butter

1 dozen eggs

1 tablespoon vanilla

8 teaspoons baking soda

18 cups oatmeal
  (a 2-pound, 10-ounce box)

1 pound M&M's candies

1 pound chocolate chips

Combine first 7 ingredients. Mix very well. Add last 3 ingredients. Mix well. Make each cookie from dough about the size of a golf ball, then flatten out by hand.

Bake at 350° for 10 to 15 minutes, depending on size of cookie.

Note: The source of this recipe is a mother who makes the dough at home, takes it to the cabin, and bakes a few dozen cookies at a time. They are large and filling. The dough keeps well in the refrigerator for quite a while. On your first try, you might want to make half the recipe.

No-Bake Peanut Butter Drops

1 cup sugar

¼ cup margarine

¼ cup milk

1½ cups quick-cooking oatmeal

2½ tablespoons creamy peanut butter

¼ cup chopped nuts

½ teaspoon vanilla

Combine sugar, margarine and milk in saucepan. Boil for 1 minute. Pour, while hot, over oatmeal and peanut butter. Add nuts and vanilla. Mix. Drop by teaspoonful onto wax paper. Let stand until firm.

Snickerdoodles

1 cup soft shortening

1½ cups sugar

2 eggs, beaten

2¾ cups flour

2 teaspoons cream of tartar

1 teaspoon baking soda

½ teaspoon salt

3 tablespoons sugar

3 teaspoons cinnamon

Mix shortening, 1½ cups sugar and eggs. Sift flour, cream of tartar, soda and salt. Add to first mixture. Chill.

Mix 3 tablespoons sugar and cinnamon. Roll dough into balls the size of a small walnut. Roll in sugar-cinnamon mixture. Place about 2 inches apart on ungreased cookie sheet.

Bake at 400° for 8 to 10 minutes. Cookies should be lightly browned, but still soft.

Makes about 5 dozen.

Nut Goody Bars

You don't need an oven for these unbaked goodies.

1 12-ounce package
chocolate chips

1 12-ounce package
butterscotch chips

1 cup peanut butter

1 10½-ounce package
miniature marshmallows

1 12-ounce can
cocktail peanuts

Combine and melt first
3 ingredients. Cool slightly.
Add marshmallows and
peanuts. Spread in a
9-by-13-inch pan. Cool. Cut.

Sour Cream Raisin Bars

Travels well.

2 cups raisins

1 cup brown sugar

1 cup butter

1⅓ cups quick-cooking
oatmeal

1 teaspoon baking soda

1¾ cups flour

3 egg yolks

1½ cups sour cream

1 cup sugar

2½ tablespoons cornstarch

1 teaspoon vanilla

Cook raisins in small amount
of water for 10 minutes. Drain
and cool. Cream brown sugar
and butter. Add oatmeal, soda
and flour. Put half the mixture
in a 9-by-13-inch pan.

Bake at 350° for 7 minutes. In
a saucepan, mix egg yolks, sour
cream, sugar and cornstarch.
Simmer, stirring constantly.
Add raisins and vanilla. Pour
over baked crust. Crumble remaining oatmeal mixture over
top. Bake 30 minutes more.

Mixed Nut Bars
These are delicious!

1½ cups flour
½ cup butter
¾ cup brown sugar
Dash of salt
2 cups mixed nuts
½ cup light corn syrup
1 cup butterscotch chips
2 tablespoons butter

Mix and pat flour, butter, brown sugar and salt into ungreased 9-by-13-inch pan.

Bake for 10 minutes at 350°. Sprinkle nuts over crust. Melt syrup, chips and butter. Pour over nuts.

Bake for 10 minutes more. Cut. Chill. Store in refrigerator.

Mounds-Type Bars
Chocolate chips, in any form, are a family favorite.

2 cups crushed
  graham crackers
⅓ cup sugar
½ cup melted butter
1 package flaked coconut
1 can sweetened
  condensed milk
1 12-ounce bag
  chocolate chips

Mix the crackers, sugar and butter. Press into a 9-by-13-inch buttered pan. Sprinkle coconut over crust. Pour milk over coconut.

Bake at 350° for 15 to 20 minutes (top should be slightly brown). Melt the chocolate chips over low heat. Spread on warm bars.

Lemon Bars

2 cups flour
1 cup butter or margarine
1½ cups powdered sugar
4 eggs, slightly beaten
2 cups sugar
4 tablespoons flour
1 teaspoon baking powder
6 tablespoons lemon juice

Heat oven to 350°. Mix the flour, butter and sugar until crumbly. Pat mixture into a 9-by-13-inch pan.

Bake for 20 minutes. Mix the remaining ingredients. Pour over the cooled baked crust.

Bake for 30 minutes more. Cool. Sprinkle with powdered sugar.

Makes 24 bars.

Lazy Day Bars

½ cup margarine or butter
1½ cups graham cracker crumbs
1 14-ounce can sweetened condensed milk
1 6-ounce package chocolate chips
1 3½-ounce can (1⅓ cups) flaked coconut
1 cup chopped nuts

In a 9-by-13-inch baking pan, melt margarine in oven. Sprinkle crumbs over margarine. Pour sweetened condensed milk evenly over crumbs. Top evenly with remaining ingredients; press down gently.

Bake at 350° (325° for a glass pan) for 25 to 30 minutes or until lightly browned. Cool thoroughly before cutting. Store, loosely covered, at room temperature.

Makes 24 bars.

Corn Flake Bars
Keeps well in the refrigerator.

4 cups corn flakes

1 cup coconut

⅓ cup slivered almonds

8 ounces marshmallows

⅓ cup margarine

1 8-ounce milk chocolate
candy bar

Combine corn flakes, coconut and almonds in a 9-by-13-inch pan. Warm in a 250° oven. Melt marshmallows and margarine. Combine corn flake mixture with marsh-mallow mixture.

Pat into 9-by-13-inch pan. Melt the chocolate bar. Spread over top. Cut into squares.

Carrot Bars

1 15-ounce jar (1⅔ cups)
applesauce

3 eggs

⅓ cup vegetable oil

1 box Carrot 'n Spice
cake mix

1 cup raisins

Topping
1 can cream cheese frosting

½ cup chopped nuts
(optional)

In large bowl, blend applesauce, eggs and oil. Mix for 1 minute at low speed. Add cake mix. Blend until moistened, then beat for 2 minutes at medium speed. Stir in raisins. Spread in greased and floured 10-by-15-inch pan or in two 8- or 9-inch-square pans.

Bake at 350° for 25 to 35 minutes, or until toothpick comes out clean. Cool.

Spread frosting over bars. Sprinkle with nuts. These bars are best if refrigerated.

Angel Food Bars

Soooo easy and soooo good!

1 box angel food cake mix
    (1-step type)
1 can lemon pie filling
1 cup flaked coconut

Glaze
2 cups powdered sugar, sifted
Juice from small lemon
Milk

Combine dry cake mix and pie filling. Beat for about 5 minutes. Add coconut. Mix well. Pour into jelly roll pan or 9-by-13-inch pan, which has been greased and floured.

Bake at 350° for 20 to 25 minutes.

Mix powdered sugar and lemon juice. Add enough milk (a teaspoon at a time) to make a rather thin glaze. When bars are cool, spread the glaze on top.

Graham Cracker Bars

Graham crackers
1 cup brown sugar
1 cup butter
½–1 cup chopped nuts
    (walnuts, pecans or
    sliced almonds)
1 cup milk chocolate chips
    (optional)

Line brownie pan (10-by-15-inch) with foil. Cover with graham crackers. Combine brown sugar and butter. Boil for 2 minutes. Pour over crackers. Sprinkle with nuts and chocolate chips.

Bake at 350° for 5 minutes. Remove each cracker from pan and place on wax paper.

Cream Cheese Bars

1 stick (½ cup) butter
or margarine

1 box yellow cake mix
(without pudding added)

1 egg

1 box powdered sugar

1 teaspoon vanilla

1 8-ounce package cream
cheese, softened

2 eggs

Preheat oven to 300°. Melt butter in 9-by-13-inch pan in the preheating oven. Pour melted butter into mixing bowl, leaving cake pan "greased." Combine cake mix, egg and melted butter. Mix well. Pat into cake pan. On low speed, mix the powdered sugar, vanilla, cream cheese and 2 eggs. Pour over base.

Bake for 45 to 50 minutes, until top is golden brown.

Pumpkin Bars

2 cups flour

2 teaspoons baking powder

1 teaspoon baking soda

½ teaspoon salt

2 teaspoons cinnamon

2 cups sugar

4 eggs, beaten

1 15-ounce can pumpkin

1 cup vegetable oil

Cream Cheese Frosting
3 ounces cream cheese,
softened

6 tablespoons butter

1 teaspoon milk

1 teaspoon vanilla

1¼ cup powdered sugar

Sift together dry ingredients. Add beaten eggs, pumpkin and oil.

Bake in jelly roll pan at 350° for 25 minutes.

Blend all frosting ingredients. Spread on cake.

Salty Nut Bars

The saltiness and sweetness is a great combination!

1½ cups flour

¾ cup brown sugar

½ teaspoon salt

½ cup butter or margarine

1 12-ounce can mixed
salted nuts or peanuts

Butterscotch Topping
1 12-ounce package
butterscotch chips

½ cup light corn syrup

2 tablespoons butter

1 teaspoon vanilla

Mix first 4 ingredients with a pastry blender. Pat into 9-by-13-inch buttered, or nonstick, pan.

Bake for 10 minutes at 350°. Sprinkle nuts over baked layer.

Melt butterscotch topping ingredients over low heat, stirring constantly. Spread over nuts.

Bake for 10 minutes at 350°. Cut into squares while still a little warm.

Candy Bar Bars

4 cups oatmeal

1 cup brown sugar

⅔ cup butter

½ cup light corn syrup

2 teaspoons vanilla

1 cup (6 ounces)
chocolate chips

⅔ cup peanut butter

Mix oatmeal and brown sugar. Melt butter and corn syrup. Add vanilla. Combine two mixtures. Pat into 9-by-13-inch pan.

Bake at 375° for 10 to 12 minutes. Cool. Melt chips and peanut butter. Spread on bars.

Speedy Little Devils

½ cup margarine or butter, melted

1 Duncan Hines Deluxe II Devils Food cake mix

¾ cup creamy peanut butter

1 7- or 7½-ounce jar marshmallow crème

Combine melted butter and dry cake mix. Reserve 1½ cups of this mixture for top crust. Pat remaining mixture into ungreased 9-by-13-inch pan. Top with combined peanut butter and marshmallow crème, and spread evenly over first layer. Crumble remaining mixture over that.

Bake for 20 minutes at 350°. Cool.

Makes 3 dozen bars.

Chocolate Scotcheroos

1 cup sugar

1 cup light corn syrup

1 cup peanut butter

6 cups Rice Krispies

1 6-ounce package chocolate chips

1 6-ounce package butterscotch chips

Combine sugar and syrup in a 3-quart saucepan. Cook over low heat, stirring constantly, just until mixture boils. Remove from heat. Blend in peanut butter. Stir in Rice Krispies. Press into buttered 9-by-13-inch pan. Melt the chips over hot water. Spread on top. Cut into 30 bars.

Marble Squares

A favorite of our daughters for potluck at the cabin. Stays moist.

8 ounces cream cheese

⅓ cup sugar

1 egg

½ cup margarine

¾ cup water

1½ 1-ounce squares
   unsweetened chocolate

2 cups flour

2 cups sugar

2 eggs

½ cup (4 ounces) sour cream

1 cup (6 ounces)
   chocolate chips

1 teaspoon baking soda

½ teaspoon salt

Combine softened cream cheese and sugar, mixing until well blended. Add egg. Mix well. Combine margarine, water and chocolate squares in saucepan. Bring to a boil. Remove from heat. Stir in combined flour and sugar. Add eggs, sour cream, baking soda and salt. Mix well.

Pour into greased and floured 15½-by-10½-inch jelly roll pan. Spoon cheese mixture over chocolate batter. Cut through batter with a knife several times for marble effect. Sprinkle with chocolate chips.

Bake at 375° for 25 to 30 minutes. Cut into squares.

Caramel Layer Chocolate Squares

Travels beautifully, if there are any left when you leave home.

1 package Kraft caramels

1 5.3-ounce can
evaporated milk, divided

1 German chocolate cake mix

¾ cup butter or margarine,
melted

1 cup chopped nuts

1 cup chocolate chips

In saucepan, combine caramels and ⅓ cup milk (half of the can). Cook over low heat, stirring until melted. Set aside. Grease and flour 9-by-13-inch pan. In large bowl, combine cake mix, butter, ⅓ cup milk and nuts. By hand, stir the dough until it holds together. Press ½ of dough into pan.

Bake at 350° for 6 minutes. Remove from oven. Sprinkle with chocolate chips. Spread caramel mixture over chips. Spread rest of dough over caramels.

Bake 15 to 18 minutes. Cool in refrigerator for 30 minutes, or overnight.

Caramel Krispies

Unwrap the caramels while sitting on the dock.

1 14-ounce bag
  Kraft caramels

3 tablespoons water

5 cups Rice Krispies

1 cup peanuts

1 cup chocolate chips

1 cup butterscotch chips

Melt caramels with water in saucepan over low heat. Stir frequently, until sauce is smooth. Pour over cereal and nuts. Toss until well coated. With greased fingers, press mixture into a greased 9-by-13-inch pan. Sprinkle chips on top.

Place in 200° oven for 5 minutes or until chips soften. Spread chips until blended to form frosting. Cool for at least 10 minutes.

Cut into bars.

Walnut Shortbread Squares

1 pound (2 cups)
   butter, softened

1 cup sugar

1 cup walnut pieces,
   coarsely ground

2 teaspoons vanilla

¼ teaspoon salt

4 cups flour, sifted

Cream butter and sugar until light and fluffy. Beat the walnuts, vanilla and salt into the creamed mixture. Add the flour. Mix well. Spoon the dough into a lightly greased jelly roll pan (10-by-15½-inch) and smooth it out, as dough will not change shape as it bakes.

Bake at 325° for about 45 minutes, or until lightly browned. Cool in pan. Cut into bars. Store in covered container. Keeps well for weeks.

Makes about 75 1-by-2-inch bars.

No-Bake Brownies

No oven? No problem!

1 cup chopped walnuts

4 cups graham cracker crumbs

½ cup sifted powdered sugar

2 tablespoons dry instant coffee

12 ounces semi-sweet chocolate chips

1 cup evaporated milk

1 teaspoon vanilla

Combine walnuts, crumbs and sugar in large bowl. Heat the coffee, chocolate chips and milk over low heat. Stir constantly until smoothly blended. Remove from heat. Add vanilla. Reserve ½ cup of chocolate mixture. Mix remaining chocolate with crumb mixture. Spread evenly in well-buttered 9-by-9-inch pan. Spread reserved chocolate mixture over top for glaze.

Chill until ready to serve. Keep refrigerated.

Makes 32 bars.

Blond Brownies

⅓ cup butter

1 cup brown sugar

2 eggs

1 teaspoon vanilla

½ cup walnuts

½ cup chocolate chips

1 cup sifted flour

½ teaspoon baking powder

⅛ teaspoon baking soda

½ teaspoon salt

Cream butter and sugar. Add remaining ingredients. Mix. Pour into a greased and floured 9-by-9-inch pan.

Bake at 350° for 20 to 25 minutes. For a double recipe, use a 9-by-13-inch pan, and bake for 30 minutes.

Makes 18 bars.

Cream Cheese Brownies

These delicious brownies have a mix as the base.

Brown layer

1 chocolate brownie mix

¼ cup vegetable oil

2 or 3 eggs (depending upon box directions)

1 teaspoon almond extract

White layer

4 tablespoons butter

8 ounces cream cheese

1½ cups sugar

2 eggs

2 tablespoons flour

1 teaspoon vanilla

Follow directions on box for cake-like brownies, adding 1 teaspoon almond extract. Spread in 9-by-13-inch pan.

Cream butter and cream cheese. Blend in all other white layer ingredients. Zigzag cream cheese mixture through the brownie mixture, using a knife or fork.

Bake at 350° for 35 minutes.

Hershey's Chocolate Brownies

A moist brownie for chocolate lovers.

½ cup (1 stick) butter
or margarine

1 cup sugar

1 can (1 pound)
Hershey's syrup

1 cup flour

4 eggs

½ teaspoon salt

1 teaspoon vanilla

¾ cup chopped nuts

Frosting
1 cup sugar

4 tablespoons (½ stick) butter

¼ cup milk

½ cup chocolate chips

Cream shortening and sugar. Add remaining brownie ingredients. Mix well—for about 4 minutes. Spread on an 11-by-16-inch jelly roll pan.

Bake at 350° for 20 minutes, or until done.

Boil sugar, butter and milk for 1 minute. Remove from heat Add chocolate chips. Stir until smooth. Immediately spread on brownies.

Kay's Chocolate Fudge

2 cups sugar

1 5.3-ounce can
evaporated milk

10 regular-sized
marshmallows

1 6-ounce package
chocolate chips

¼ pound (1 stick) butter,
cut up

1 teaspoon vanilla

Combine sugar, milk and marshmallows in a heavy pan. Bring to a boil, stirring constantly. Pour over chocolate chips, butter and vanilla, mixing well. Pour into 9-by-9-inch pan. Cool. Refrigerate.

Chocolate Candies

Enjoy directly from the freezer!

2 squares unsweetened
  baking chocolate

1 can sweetened
  condensed milk

Dash of salt

1 teaspoon vanilla

Crushed nutmeats and/or
  flaked coconut

Mix chocolate, milk and salt together. Stir over low heat until thick. Add vanilla, and let cool somewhat, stirring occasionally.

Before it cools completely, roll into small balls, and roll in nutmeats or coconut. Refrigerate.

S'mores

Fun around the fireplace or campfire.
The name S'mores comes from "you want some more?"

Graham crackers

Marshmallows

Milk chocolate candy bars

Place a cracker-sized piece of chocolate on graham cracker. Toast a marshmallow over the coals in the fireplace or the campfire. Put toasted marshmallow on chocolate. Top with second graham cracker.

Beverages

Fruit Crush

The base for this refreshing summer drink may be stored in your freezer until needed. Great to have on hand when you're expecting company.

3 cups water

2 cups sugar

1 46-ounce can
  pineapple juice

1½ cups orange juice

¼ cup lemon juice

3 ripe bananas, mashed

3 quarts ginger ale or
  sparkling water, chilled

In a large kettle, mix water and sugar. Bring to a boil. Remove from heat. Stir in fruit juices and mashed bananas. (Bananas can be mashed in a blender or a food processor, with a small amount of juice.) Pour into 4 ice cube freezer trays. Freeze until firm. When frozen, the cubes can be put into plastic bags for easy cooler storage or transport.

To serve, take from freezer about 15 minutes before putting into glasses. Break up mixture, and fill glasses ⅓ full of fruit crush. Fill remainder of glass with ginger ale or sparkling water. Stir.

Makes 6 quarts, or 24 servings.

Cranberry Punch

1 quart cranberry juice
cocktail, chilled

2 cups pineapple juice, chilled

1½ cups sugar

2 quarts ginger ale, chilled

Combine juices with sugar. Just before serving, add ice cubes and ginger ale.

Makes 28 half-cup servings.

Mock Champagne
Easy to make for any number of people.

Apple cider or juice

Pineapple juice

Ginger ale

Combine equal parts of each ingredient. Serve over ice. The ginger ale should be a last-minute addition.

Cranberry Slush
A cooling red punch.

1 quart Ocean Spray
cranberry juice cocktail

1 12-ounce can
frozen lemonade

12 ounces (1½ cups)
bourbon

Mix all ingredients in a 1-gallon container, such as an ice cream pail. Freeze. Remove from freezer when ready to use.

Kool-Aid Punch for the Lake Crowd

1 large package cherry
Kool-Aid
1 large package strawberry
Kool-Aid
3 quarts water
2 cups sugar
1 6-ounce can frozen
orange juice
1 6-ounce can frozen
lemonade
1 quart ginger ale

Mix all ingredients, except
ginger ale, which should be
added just before serving.

Makes 48 half-cup servings.

Orange Julia

1 6-ounce can frozen
orange juice
1 cup milk
1 cup water
¼–½ cup sugar
1 teaspoon vanilla
10 ice cubes

Mix all ingredients in blender
at low speed, gradually adding
ice cubes. Blend until smooth.

Easiest Lemonade

Juice of 1 large lemon
½ cup sugar
1 quart water

Mix. Chill. Serve over
ice cubes.

Wine Cooler

A good refresher for a summer day.

Red wine
Seven-Up
Ice cubes

Choose your favorite red wine—Rose, Pink Chablis, Burgundy or Cold Duck. Place ice cubes in a tall glass. Fill ½ with wine and ½ with Seven-Up.

Root Beer Float

For a cool treat on a hot day, remember the root beer float. Put vanilla ice cream in a tall glass, fill with root beer, and enjoy!

Ginger Tea

A refreshing, cool drink.

3 tea bags
1 cup boiling water
Juice of 2 oranges
Juice of 2 lemons
½ cup sugar
1 28-ounce bottle ginger ale, chilled

Make a cup of strong tea by putting 3 tea bags into 1 cup boiling water. Remove bags. Add fruit juices and sugar.

Chill. Just before serving, add ginger ale.

Makes about 5 8-ounce servings.

Friendship Tea Mix

Although usually a hot drink,
try mixing this with cold water during warm weather.

1 cup instant tea

1 14-ounce jar powdered
  orange breakfast drink

2 3-ounce packages
  lemonade mix

1½ cups sugar

2 teaspoons ground cloves

2 teaspoons cinnamon

Combine all ingredients. Mix well. To serve, put 2 teaspoons of mix into cup. Fill with boiling water.

Sun Tea

This tea will not be bitter or cloudy, and will keep well for days.
Experiment with different flavors of tea.

Fill a 2-quart glass jar with cold water. Put 2 or 3 tea bags in jar, with tags hanging on outside. Screw on cover. Put out in the sun for 4 to 6 hours. Chill and serve over ice.

Cocoa Mix

8-quart package dry milk

1-pound can Nestle's Quik

6-ounce jar non-dairy creamer

1 cup powdered sugar

¼ teaspoon salt

Mix all ingredients. Store in tightly covered container (an ice cream bucket works well).

To serve, mix 1 part cocoa mix to 2 parts hot water.

Margie's Mist

Similar to a very famous liqueur.

10 ounces water

1¼ cups sugar

14 ounces vodka

6 heaping tablespoons
  Ovaltine

Drop of rum extract

1 pint whipping cream

Simmer water and sugar. Cool. Mix remaining ingredients with water and sugar mixture in a 2-quart container. Store in refrigerator. Shake well before serving.

Hot Buttered Rum Mix

A winter recipe to enjoy on a snowy day, by a crackling fire.

¼ pound (1 stick) butter,
  softened

1 pound dark brown sugar

¼ teaspoon cinnamon

¼ teaspoon nutmeg

¼ teaspoon cloves

Rum

Cream butter and sugar. Add spices. Mix well. Store in covered container in refrigerator.

To serve, put 1 heaping tablespoon of mixture in a cup. Add 1½ ounces dark rum. Fill with boiling water. Can be garnished with a cinnamon stick and lemon.

Makes 12 to 14 servings.

Egg Coffee
An old-fashioned way to make clear, non-bitter coffee.

Water

Coffee, regular or coarsely ground

1 egg, beaten or shaken up in a small, covered jar

Stove-top coffee pot (campers may use a covered kettle)

Fill coffee pot ½ to ¾ full of water. Bring to a boil. In a small bowl, place 1 scant tablespoon of dry coffee for each cup of water used. Pour enough beaten egg into the coffee to thoroughly moisten the grounds when mixed together with a fork. Stir moistened coffee into boiling water.

Have it boil up, but not over (hence the partially filled coffee pot). Turn down heat, and allow coffee to brew for several minutes. If you want a full pot of coffee, boil more water, and add to coffee pot. Pour about ½ cup cold water into pot to settle the grounds. Coffee may be kept warm on low heat. Store remaining egg in a jar for future use.

Potpourri

Best Ever Fudge Sauce

Serve hot or cold.

1 6-ounce package
 chocolate chips

½ cup butter

2 cups powdered sugar, sifted

1⅓ cups evaporated milk

1 teaspoon vanilla

Melt chocolate and butter. Remove from heat. Add sugar and milk. Blend. Bring to a boil, stirring constantly. Cook and stir for about 8 minutes. Add vanilla.

Serve warm over ice cream. Store in covered container in refrigerator. Keeps forever!

Fabulous Fudge Sauce

1 12-ounce package
 chocolate chips

1 cup miniature
 marshmallows

1 14-ounce can sweetened
 condensed milk

½ cup milk

1 teaspoon vanilla

Combine all ingredients. Heat slowly over low heat, until chips and marshmallows are melted. Stir occasionally.

Cool and refrigerate. May reheat for serving.

Tops 15 to 20 sundaes.

Butterscotch Sauce

Do not freeze. Keeps about 3 weeks in the refrigerator.

1 pound dark brown sugar

1 cup sugar

1 cup half-and-half

1 stick butter

2 teaspoons vanilla

Combine all ingredients in top of double boiler. Cook slowly, until thick.

Tops about 12 sundaes.

Cinnamon Blueberry Sauce

Serve warm over waffles, pancakes or French toast.

½ cup sugar

4 teaspoons cornstarch

½ teaspoon grated lemon peel

¼ teaspoon cinnamon

Dash of salt

⅔ cup water

1 10-ounce package frozen blueberries, thawed, divided

1 teaspoon lemon juice

In a small bowl, combine sugar, cornstarch, lemon peel, cinnamon and salt. Set aside.

In saucepan, combine the water and ½ cup of the blueberries. Bring to a boil and mash berries. Add sugar mixture, cook and stir, until sauce thickens and bubbles. Add remaining blueberries and lemon juice. Simmer 3 to 5 minutes more.

Makes 2 cups.

Strawberry Topping for Pancakes or French Toast

8 ounces cream cheese, softened

1 stick unsalted butter

½–¾ cup powdered sugar

1 teaspoon vanilla

8 good-sized strawberries, mashed

Combine all ingredients. Mix well. Store in refrigerator.

Strawberry or Raspberry Jam for Freezer

3 cups fresh berries, mashed
5 cups sugar
1 package powdered pectin
1 cup water

Wash, hull and mash berries. Add sugar. Mix well. Let stand for about 15 minutes, stirring occasionally.

Dissolve pectin in water, and boil for 1 minute. Add water mixture to fruit. Stir for 2 minutes. Pour into freezer containers, cover and let stand until jelled. Freeze.

This will also keep well in the refrigerator for 1 month. May also be used as a topping for ice cream or pound cake.

Fresh Strawberry Topping

Clean and cut up fresh strawberries. Sprinkle lightly with sugar, until it suits your taste of sweetness. Chill for several hours or overnight.

Use as a topping for ice cream, shortcake, pound cake, angel food cake, pancakes, etc. You may choose to use it in combination with slightly sweetened whipped cream.

Rhubarb Freezer Jam

2 cups rhubarb

1 cup sugar

1 3-ounce package wild strawberry JELL-O

1 8-ounce can crushed pineapple, plus liquid

Cook rhubarb and sugar until soft. Add JELL-O, pineapple and liquid.

Bring to a boil. Simmer for 15 minutes. Pour into sterilized jars. Freeze.

Orange Sauce for Wild Game
Serve over duck or goose.

1 cup orange marmalade

½ cup orange juice

2 tablespoons freshly grated orange peel

2 tablespoons orange-flavored liqueur

Combine all ingredients in a small saucepan.

Heat over low heat, stirring until smooth.

Parmesan Croutons
A good way to use up extra bread.

8 slices bread

¼ cup butter or margarine, melted

¼ cup grated Parmesan cheese

Remove crusts and cube bread. Toss with melted butter and Parmesan cheese. Place on baking sheet.

Bake at 375° for about 10 minutes. When cool, store in airtight container.

Barbecue Sauce

3 garlic cloves

2 tablespoons margarine

1 cup ketchup

¼ cup water

2 tablespoons brown sugar

2 teaspoons liquid smoke

1 tablespoon
   Worcestershire sauce

½ teaspoon salt

¼ teaspoon pepper

Slice garlic cloves; brown in margarine and discard garlic. Add remaining ingredients. Simmer for 10 minutes.

Makes 1½ cups.

Best Barbecue Sauce
Use extra sauce as a hostess gift!

1 medium onion, chopped

⅓ cup butter or margarine,
   melted

¾ cup brown sugar

12 ounces mustard

2 ounces (¼ cup)
   liquid smoke

1 tablespoon garlic powder

1 26-ounce bottle ketchup

½ cup (scant)
   Worcestershire sauce

⅓ cup lemon juice

2½ cups water

Sauté onion in butter in large saucepan. Add brown sugar. Mix well. Add remaining ingredients. Bring to a boil, and simmer for 30 minutes, stirring occasionally.

Store in refrigerator. Keeps well for a long time. Delicious for hamburgers, ribs, chicken, brisket, steak, etc. Recipe doubles easily.

Makes 2 quarts.

Hamburger To Go

Before heading for vacation, brown a large amount of hamburger with chopped onion and seasonings. Divide into usable portions and freeze. It can serve as "ice" in the cooler enroute to your destination. Thaw, as needed, for chili, sloppy joes, lasagna, taco salad, stroganoff, spaghetti, taco pie, soup or casseroles.

Bacon To Go

Fry a pound, or more, of bacon. Drain on paper towels. Wrap in foil and freeze. Thaw, as needed, for use with BLTs (bacon, lettuce, tomato sandwiches), poached eggs supreme, tossed salads, scrambled eggs or pancake batter. To serve hot, as with eggs, place under broiler or in hot frying pan for a few minutes.

Index

Contributors of Recipes

Peggy Alberg
Esther Allen
Ginny Anderson
Lois Anderson
Gail Barduson
Dorothy Boen
Betty Bordwell
Lola Brubacher
Olga Brubacher
Sara Brubacher
Faye Burke
Kay Burke
Sandy Burke
Mildred Burke
Hazel Cannon
Janet Carlson
Billie Cashman
Mary Choinere
Marge Coppins
Jo Crisman
Liz Cullen
Nancy Damerow
Bette Dedon
Terry Dee
Rosemary Dineen
Kathy Dirks
Eleanor Donaghy
Marie Edstrom
Georgiana Ehrlichmann
Lynn Empanger
Barb Engmark
Ole Enli
Miriam Erdahl
Char Erickson
Mary Ernst
Marian Ertl
Joyce Fargo
Kitty Felion
Michelle Felion
Margaret Feudner
Bonnie Fischer
Gerry Fleming
Trudy Forster
Bev Gerber
Barb Graf
Lucy Grams

Judy Grothe
Donna Gustafson
Francis Gustafson
Evy Hagen
Laurie Halter
Marian Hart
Jean Helgeson
Ruth Hopperstad
Gladys Jacobson
Howard Jacobson
Norma Jacobson
Larry Jeffery
Carol Johnson
Helen Johnson
Louise Jones
Betty Keunzli
Betty Kidder
Mice Kilby
Joe Knoblauch
Lorraine Knoblauch
LuAnne Knoblauch
Mary Knoblauch
Carolyn Krautkremer
Elaine Krenik
Carolyn Latz
Marilyn Lehman
Nola Lockwood
Helene Lohmann
Audrey Lommen
Sharon Magnuson
Ann Mark
Doris Maser
Elaine May
Ann McCormick
Michael McCuddin
Carol Mereness
Janine Merrick
Virginia Merrick
Kathy Mimnaugh
Alice Mol
Mona Nagel
Barb Nelson
Mary Nelson
Bernice Ness
Mary Niemann
Audrey Novak

Ruth Novotny
Marlene Olseth
Nancy Olseth
Clara Olson
Ginger Overbye
Ethel Payne
Bob Paul
Ruby Perkins
Kay Peterson
Lucille Petrak
Carol Pohle
June Raarup
Diane Rabe
Susie Redpath
Lea Rae Reese
Carolyn Ring
Jo Roseborough
Joan Ryberg
Lynne Segal
Anne Senn
Pat Shearer
Bobbie Shoemaker
Nikki Sindt
Betsy Skjervold
Dianne E. Smith
Mary Ellen Solberg
Judy Sotebeer Sharon
Stefan Mary Straka
Gail Swalve
Pat Tagader
Irene Tanglen
Bev Thurn
Vi Towley
Carol Tveit
Shirley Velner
Lorraine Wagner
Dawn Wanous
Diana Waterbury
Perry Wegleitner
Sue Weinstein
Dorothy Welch
Carol Wentzlaff
Aileen Wigginton
Mary Lou Williams
Peg Wilhoit
Carol Witsoe

About the Authors

Margie Knoblauch was a Minnesota native who lived in the Minnetonka-Hopkins area of the Twin Cities. A wife and the mother of six children, she spent her summers at the family's log cabin, "Knobby Pines," near Park Rapids, Minnesota.

Margie was a University of Minnesota home economics graduate with a degree in institutional management, and she worked as a home economist for Northern States Power Company and as a representative of Admiral Corporation. She was a member of Home Economics in Homemaking, a group of home economics graduates and was involved in marketing a cookbook for that group.

Margie's family has been involved in several food-and-beverage establishments in Minnesota, including the Hopkins House and Breezy Point Resort.

Mary Brubacher, a resident of Hopkins, Minnesota, has had a long-time interest in collecting recipes and cookbooks and preparing special foods. She has also helped produce a cookbook for a women's group in Hopkins.

A wife and the mother of three daughters, Mary has been a "cabin person" at Little Hubert Lake, near Nisswa, Minnesota. She is a graduate of Hamline University, with a bachelor's degree in nursing, and was a school nurse in the Hopkins School District.